CANNING & PRESERVING TECHNIQUES BIBLE

Isaiah Schwartz

TABLE OF CONTENT

Chapter 1: Amish Canning Techniques 5
- Essential Tools and Equipment 5
- Selecting and Preparing Jars, Lids, and Bands 12
- Practical Tips for Water-Bath Canning 15
- Safe Pressure Canning Made Easy 20
- Troubleshooting Common Canning Problems 25
- Storage Advice for Your Canned Foods 30

Chapter 2: Amish Curing Methods for Meat 35
- Choosing and Preparing Meat for Curing 35
- Easy Salt and Sugar Curing Mixtures 40
- Step-by-Step Guide to Dry Curing at Home 44
- Common Mistakes and How to Avoid Them 50
- Practical Storage Tips for Cured Meats 54

Chapter 3: Amish Smoking Essentials 58
- Building a Simple Amish-Style Smokehouse 58
- Selecting the Right Wood for Best Flavor 68
- Hot Smoking vs. Cold Smoking: A Practical Guide 72
- Smoking Meat, Fish, and Cheese Successfully 77
- Tips to Perfect Your Smoking Techniques 83

Chapter 4: Amish Pickling and Fermenting 88
- How to Make Perfect Pickling Brines 88
- Practical Recipes for Quick Pickles 94
- Easy Fermented Vegetables Step-by-Step 99
- Sauerkraut the Amish Way 109
- Common Issues in Pickling and How to Solve Them 114
- Best Practices for Storing Pickled and Fermented Foods 119

Chapter 5: Amish Methods for Drying Foods 123
- Simple Outdoor and Indoor Drying Setups 123
- Best Techniques for Drying Fruits, Vegetables, and Herbs 129
- Common Drying Mistakes and Solutions 135
- Practical Storage Tips for Dried Goods 140

Chapter 6: Amish Root Cellaring Basics 145
- How to Build and Organize a Simple Root Cellar 145
- Ideal Conditions for Long-Term Storage 154

Ideal Conditions for Long-Term Storage 158
Practical Advice for Storing Root Vegetables and Fruits....................................162
Tips to Prevent Spoilage and Extend Storage Life...167
Common Root Cellar Problems and Solutions..172

CHAPTER 1: AMISH CANNING TECHNIQUES

Essential Tools and Equipment

In Amish homes, canning isn't just a seasonal chore—it's a way of life, a tradition passed down through generations, essential for ensuring a pantry filled with nutritious foods year-round. Successful canning begins with the right tools and equipment, carefully chosen and maintained to last a lifetime. As someone raised within an Amish community, I've learned the importance of simplicity, durability, and efficiency. Below, I'll guide you through the essential tools that every Amish kitchen relies on for successful food preservation.

1. Canning Jars

First and foremost, reliable canning jars form the foundation of safe food preservation. Mason jars—such as those made by Ball or Kerr—are the traditional choice due to their proven durability. Glass jars come in several sizes, but the three most essential are:

- **Quart jars** (32 oz): Best suited for whole fruits, tomatoes, sauces, soups, and larger batches of vegetables.

- **Pint jars** (16 oz): Ideal for jams, jellies, relishes, pickles, and smaller servings of vegetables or meats.

- **Half-pint jars** (8 oz): Perfect for preserves, marmalades, sauces, or specialty condiments.

Choose jars specifically designed for canning, ensuring they are free of cracks, chips, or imperfections that could compromise safety.

2. Lids and Bands

Canning lids come in two parts: a metal lid with a sealing compound on its underside, and a screw-on metal band. The lid ensures an airtight seal, while the band secures the lid during processing. Always purchase new lids each year—used lids rarely seal reliably a second time—while bands can be reused as long as they're rust-free and undamaged.

3. Water-Bath Canner

For canning high-acid foods like fruits, pickles, jams, and tomatoes, a water-bath canner is indispensable. A typical Amish kitchen uses a large enamel-coated steel pot with a removable wire rack to hold jars upright and away from direct heat. The rack prevents jars from bumping and cracking during processing. Ensure the canner is deep enough to cover jars by at least one inch of boiling water during processing.

4. Pressure Canner

Low-acid foods like green beans, corn, potatoes, meats, and soups require pressure canning to safely eliminate harmful bacteria such as botulism spores. Amish families prefer sturdy, high-quality pressure canners, typically made of heavy-gauge aluminum. Models such as All American or Presto are common choices for their reliability and simplicity. Always choose a model with a clearly visible pressure gauge or weighted regulator to maintain correct pressure levels.

5. Jar Funnel

An inexpensive yet invaluable tool, the wide-mouth jar funnel makes filling jars clean, quick, and efficient. Amish kitchens commonly use stainless steel funnels for durability, ease of cleaning, and longevity.

6. Jar Lifter

Safety is paramount when handling hot jars during the canning process. A jar lifter is designed specifically to grasp hot jars securely and transfer them in and out of boiling water or a pressure canner safely. Choose one with sturdy, heat-resistant grips.

7. Lid Magnet

A small yet practical tool, the lid magnet helps retrieve sterilized lids from hot water without contaminating them. Although not strictly necessary, Amish families appreciate how this simple gadget improves cleanliness and convenience.

8. Bubble Remover and Headspace Tool

This small plastic or wooden utensil helps eliminate trapped air bubbles in filled jars, ensuring proper sealing and food safety. The opposite end usually has markings indicating recommended headspace (the gap between food and lid), simplifying measurements.

9. Clean Cloths and Towels

Always have several clean, lint-free cloths on hand. Use them to wipe jar rims thoroughly after filling, ensuring a perfect seal. Additionally, thick kitchen towels are invaluable for setting hot jars on countertops, reducing sudden temperature changes that could crack the glass.

10. Timer

Accurate timing is critical in canning. Amish cooks rely on simple mechanical kitchen timers, though modern digital timers are equally effective. Whichever you choose, ensure it's reliable, clear, and easy to read.

11. Labels and Markers

Clearly labeling jars with the contents and date of preservation helps you rotate your pantry stock, ensuring freshness and quality. Permanent markers and adhesive labels or simple masking tape are the Amish choice for practicality.

Practical Amish Wisdom—A Note on Equipment Care:

- Always clean and sterilize your equipment thoroughly before and after use to ensure safety and longevity.
- Inspect jars regularly for imperfections; Amish wisdom teaches that one compromised jar can spoil the entire batch.
- Maintain and check your pressure canner annually; proper care ensures decades of reliable service.

With these simple yet essential tools, you're ready to continue the legacy of Amish food preservation, ensuring your family's table remains rich with wholesome, preserved foods throughout every season.

Selecting and Preparing Jars, Lids, and Bands

In Amish kitchens, attention to detail makes the difference between a safely preserved pantry full of wholesome food and jars that spoil prematurely. Properly selecting and preparing jars, lids, and bands isn't simply a task—it's a ritual rooted deeply in the traditions I was taught from childhood. Below, I'll guide you step-by-step, sharing practical Amish wisdom to ensure every jar you seal lasts safely and deliciously through the seasons.

Step 1: Selecting Your Jars

Always begin by choosing jars specifically designed for canning—commonly referred to as Mason jars. Amish families primarily rely on trusted brands like Ball or Kerr, which have proven themselves over generations.

When selecting jars, carefully examine each one for:

- **Chips or cracks**: Run your finger gently along the rim and sides of each jar to detect imperfections. Even a small chip or hairline crack can prevent sealing and spoil your food.
- **Smoothness of the rim**: The sealing surface (the top rim) must be smooth and intact for a safe, airtight seal.
- **Glass clarity**: Slight cloudiness is normal, especially if reusing jars, but significant discoloration or etching may indicate weak glass prone to cracking during processing.

Amish tip: When reusing jars, hold each one up to the light. Imperfections that are invisible at first glance can suddenly appear clearly.

Step 2: Preparing and Sterilizing Your Jars

Before filling, it's critical to ensure your jars are clean and sterilized. Although the canning process itself typically sterilizes jars, Amish tradition emphasizes extra caution, especially with jams, jellies, and high-sugar preserves.

Here's the Amish-approved way to prepare your jars:

- Wash jars thoroughly in hot, soapy water, using a long-handled brush to scrub thoroughly inside.
- Rinse jars with hot water to remove all soap residue.
- For sterilization:

- **Method 1 (Boiling):** Place jars upright in your water-bath canner, cover completely with hot water, and boil for 10 minutes. Keep jars submerged until you're ready to fill them.
- **Method 2 (Oven):** Place clean jars upright on a baking sheet in a preheated oven at 225°F (110°C) for at least 15 minutes. Keep the jars in the oven until ready to fill.
- **Method 3 (Dishwasher):** Modern Amish households may run jars through a dishwasher's sterilize cycle, timing their preparation to finish just before filling.

Amish tip: Always handle hot jars carefully—use jar lifters or clean oven mitts to prevent burns or contamination.

Step 3: Selecting and Preparing Lids

Canning lids have two parts: the flat metal lid with a sealing compound underneath and the screw-on band. Amish practice dictates that new metal lids must be used each season, as reused lids often fail to seal reliably.

When choosing lids, ensure they:

- Are specifically marked for canning.
- Show no signs of rust, damage, or discoloration.
- Have a smooth, intact sealing compound.

To prepare lids:

- Wash lids gently in warm, soapy water.
- Rinse thoroughly to remove any soap residue.
- Place lids in a saucepan of hot water (do **not** boil) for at least 5 minutes before using. Keep lids in hot water until ready to place on jars.

Important Amish reminder: Do not boil lids, as excessive heat can damage the sealing compound and prevent proper sealing.

Step 4: Checking and Preparing Bands

Bands secure lids during processing and storage. Unlike lids, bands can be reused year after year if they're undamaged and clean.

Inspect bands carefully for:

- Rust or corrosion: Rust can prevent a proper seal or contaminate food.
- Bends or dents: Bands should screw smoothly onto jars without effort.

Wash bands in warm, soapy water, rinse well, and dry thoroughly before use. Keep extra bands on hand, as Amish practicality teaches that replacements are often needed unexpectedly.

Amish tip: After jars are sealed and cooled (usually after 24 hours), you can remove bands for storage. This prevents rust formation and allows you to reuse bands longer.

Amish Secrets for Ensuring a Perfect Seal Every Time:

- Always warm your jars slightly before filling, as placing hot food into cold jars risks cracking.
- Wipe the rim of every jar meticulously with a clean, damp cloth before placing lids. Even tiny specks of food can prevent sealing.
- Do not overtighten bands—Amish tradition says tighten bands until they're comfortably finger-tight (snug but not forced). Overtightening bands can prevent air from escaping during processing and compromise your seal.

By following these practical Amish steps in selecting and preparing your jars, lids, and bands, you'll confidently preserve foods safely, knowing your pantry will offer nourishment and comfort throughout the year.

Practical Tips for Water-Bath Canning

Water-bath canning is a foundational skill in every Amish household. As a child growing up Amish, summer days were often spent alongside my mother and grandmother, carefully packing jars and listening closely as they shared practical tips for preserving jams, fruits, tomatoes, and pickles. I'll pass these secrets onto you, ensuring your food remains safe, flavorful, and perfectly preserved for seasons to come.

Tip 1: Know Your Foods
Water-bath canning is ideal for preserving high-acid foods, including:

- Fruits (peaches, pears, cherries, applesauce, berries)
- Jams, jellies, and preserves
- Pickles and relishes
- Tomatoes (though some recipes require added lemon juice or vinegar to ensure acidity)

Always verify the acidity of the foods you're preserving; if you're unsure, follow trusted recipes closely to avoid spoilage.

Tip 2: Preparing Your Water-Bath Canner

To ensure success, prepare your canner thoughtfully:

- Fill your water-bath canner halfway with hot water. Place the wire rack in the bottom.

- Heat the water gradually until it's gently simmering (about 180°F/82°C), ready to receive your filled jars.

- Make sure there's enough water to cover jars by at least one inch when submerged. Keep extra boiling water nearby in case you need to top it off during processing.

Amish Wisdom: Never place jars directly on the bottom of the pot—they may crack under intense heat. Always use a rack or folded kitchen towel to protect them.

Tip 3: Filling and Sealing Jars Properly

Accuracy at this stage ensures safe storage:

- Use your jar funnel to neatly fill jars, leaving appropriate headspace (usually ¼-inch for jams and ½-inch for fruits, pickles, and tomatoes).

- Gently remove air bubbles by running your bubble remover around the inside edges of each jar.

- Carefully wipe each jar's rim with a clean, damp cloth to guarantee a good seal.

- Place warm lids onto jars, centering them carefully, and secure bands finger-tight—snug but never overly tightened.

Tip 4: Maintaining a Proper Boil
When jars are submerged:

- Bring water to a full rolling boil quickly but gently.

- Start timing only after the water has reached a steady rolling boil.

- Maintain a consistent boil throughout the entire recommended processing time. If boiling stops, restart the timing from the beginning to ensure safety.

Amish Secret: Covering your canner with a tight-fitting lid helps maintain a consistent boil and reduces processing time.

Tip 5: Accurate Timing is Essential
Timing is crucial in water-bath canning. Follow tested recipes closely, as different foods require specific processing times:

- Jams and jellies usually require 10–15 minutes.

- Fruits and tomatoes typically require 20–45 minutes, depending on jar size.

- Pickles generally need about 10–20 minutes.

Use a reliable timer, checking periodically to ensure continuous boiling.

Tip 6: Cooling Jars Properly
Proper cooling is crucial for sealing:

- After the processing time ends, turn off heat and remove the lid. Allow jars to rest in the hot water for about 5 minutes.

- Using your jar lifter, carefully remove jars from the canner, placing them upright on a folded towel or cooling rack.

- Do not tighten bands or disturb jars during cooling—this could break the seal.

- Allow jars to cool undisturbed for 12–24 hours. Listen for the satisfying "ping" indicating a successful seal.

Amish wisdom: Never place hot jars directly on cold surfaces—always use towels or racks to prevent cracking from sudden temperature changes.

Tip 7: Checking Your Seals
After cooling completely, carefully test each jar:

- Gently press the lid's center—properly sealed lids should not move or make a popping sound.

- If a jar hasn't sealed properly, refrigerate immediately and use within a week, or re-process promptly with a fresh lid.

Tip 8: Labeling and Storing Your Jars
Labeling ensures freshness and organization:

- Clearly label jars with contents and processing date.

- Store your sealed jars upright in a cool, dry, and dark place, ideally between 50–70°F (10–21°C).

- Rotate jars frequently, using older jars first.

Amish tip: Store jars without bands if humidity is high, preventing rust formation and extending band longevity.

Common Mistakes and Amish Solutions:

- **Floating fruit:**
  Gently pack fruits tightly and firmly into jars without crushing, and always fill jars with hot syrup or liquid.

- **Siphoning (loss of liquid):**
  Ensure proper headspace and avoid rapid temperature changes. Allow jars to sit briefly after processing before removing them from water.

- **Cloudy liquid:**
  Use distilled or filtered water if your tap water is hard, as minerals can cause cloudiness.

With these practical Amish tips, water-bath canning will soon feel natural and rewarding. Each successfully sealed jar not only nourishes your family but also connects you to a heritage rich in wisdom and simplicity, turning preservation into a joyful and comforting tradition.

Safe Pressure Canning Made Easy

Pressure canning is an essential method used by Amish households to safely preserve low-acid foods such as vegetables, meats, poultry, fish, and homemade soups. Though pressure canning might seem intimidating at first, my Amish upbringing taught me that with patience, practice, and attention to detail, this preservation method can become an enjoyable and straightforward process. In this section, I'll guide you step-by-step, simplifying pressure canning and sharing practical Amish insights that ensure your pantry shelves are safely stocked for months to come.

Understanding Pressure Canning

Pressure canning safely preserves foods by heating jars to temperatures above boiling (around 240°F/115°C), which is essential to eliminate harmful bacteria like Clostridium botulinum, the cause of botulism. Foods requiring pressure canning include:

- Vegetables (beans, corn, carrots, potatoes, peas)
- Meat (beef, pork, poultry)
- Seafood and fish
- Soups and stews

Always follow tested pressure canning recipes precisely to ensure food safety.

Step-by-Step Amish Guide to Safe Pressure Canning:

Step 1: Preparing Your Pressure Canner

- Begin by checking your canner thoroughly:
    - Inspect the sealing ring (if present) for cracks or wear.
    - Verify that the vent pipe is clear and unobstructed.
    - Ensure the pressure gauge or weighted regulator functions correctly.
- Add about two to three inches of hot water to your canner. Unlike water-bath canning, jars in pressure canning are not fully submerged.

Amish tip: Keep your pressure canner's manual handy and review it carefully each season. Following manufacturer instructions ensures safety and longevity.

Step 2: Filling and Preparing Jars

- Prepare foods according to trusted recipes, keeping your jars hot and ready for filling.
- Fill jars leaving recommended headspace (commonly 1 inch for vegetables, meats, and soups).
- Remove air bubbles by running a bubble remover or plastic spatula around the jar interior.
- Wipe jar rims carefully with a clean, damp cloth.
- Apply warm lids and secure bands finger-tight—firm but never overly tight.

Step 3: Loading Your Pressure Canner

- Use your jar lifter to carefully place jars onto the canner rack.
- Jars should not touch each other directly; space them evenly to allow proper steam circulation.
- Lock your canner lid securely, following the manufacturer's instructions.

Amish wisdom: Always double-check that the lid is locked properly—Amish cooks emphasize patience and precision at this critical moment.

Step 4: Venting the Pressure Canner

- Heat the canner on high heat until steam begins to steadily escape through the vent pipe.
- Allow steam to vent continuously for 10 full minutes. This step removes air and ensures proper temperature is reached inside the canner.

- After 10 minutes of steady venting, place the weighted regulator or close the vent valve (depending on your canner model).

Step 5: Reaching and Maintaining Pressure

- Allow pressure to build inside the canner until it reaches the exact pressure indicated by your recipe:
    - Typically, it's 10 pounds pressure (psi) at sea level, but higher altitudes may require adjustments (always consult your canner's manual).
- Once the proper pressure is reached, immediately adjust your stove's heat to maintain a steady, consistent pressure.
- Start timing your process only after reaching and stabilizing the required pressure.

Important Amish Reminder: If at any point your pressure drops below the recommended level, reset your timer once you've regained the correct pressure. Accuracy is vital for safety.

Step 6: Cooling and Releasing Pressure Safely

- After the processing time ends, turn off the heat and allow your canner to cool naturally. Never speed up cooling by immersing it in cold water or opening vents prematurely.
- Wait until the pressure gauge reads zero or until the weighted regulator shows no signs of pressure.
- Carefully remove the weighted regulator or open the vent valve slightly to ensure all pressure is gone.

Amish safety tip: Patience at this stage prevents accidents and ensures jar safety. Sudden depressurization may break jars or cause food siphoning.

Step 7: Removing and Cooling Jars

- After removing the lid, wait an additional 5–10 minutes before taking jars out to prevent siphoning.

- Use your jar lifter to carefully transfer jars upright to a padded surface (like a thick towel) to cool slowly, undisturbed, for at least 12–24 hours.

- Avoid retightening bands or touching lids while cooling; disturbing jars can break the seal.

Amish Troubleshooting Tips for Pressure Canning:

- **Liquid loss (siphoning):**
  Likely caused by rapid depressurization or fluctuating pressure. Maintain stable heat and proper cooldown procedures.

- **Failure to seal:**
  Often due to residue on jar rims or improperly tightened bands. Always wipe rims carefully and secure bands correctly.

- **Food discoloration or mushy texture:**
  Usually a result of over-processing or incorrect pressure. Always follow tested recipes and proper timing strictly.

Storage Advice for Pressure-Canned Foods:

- Label jars clearly with contents and canning date.

- Remove bands for storage to prevent rusting.

- Store jars in a cool, dark pantry (ideally 50–70°F or 10–21°C).
- Regularly inspect jars; discard immediately if the seal is compromised, or food appears suspicious.

Pressure canning, though initially challenging, quickly becomes a routine and rewarding practice when following these practical Amish guidelines. With careful adherence to these simple steps, your pantry shelves will soon be lined with safely preserved, nutritious food that provides comfort, health, and security year-round.

Troubleshooting Common Canning Problems

Every Amish household experiences the occasional setback during canning, despite generations of experience. Over many years spent working alongside my mother and grandmother, I learned practical solutions for common canning issues. Here, I'll share these traditional Amish troubleshooting methods clearly and practically, ensuring that your preserved goods remain safe, tasty, and of high quality every season.

Problem 1: Jars Didn't Seal Properly

An unsealed jar is a common canning headache, but easily preventable with attention to detail.

Possible Causes and Solutions:

- **Food residue on jar rims:**
  Always wipe rims meticulously with a clean, damp cloth before applying lids.

- **Incorrect headspace:**
  Follow the recommended headspace in your recipe precisely. Too little or too much headspace prevents sealing.

- **Damaged lids or jars:**
  Inspect lids carefully; use new lids every time, and discard jars with chips or imperfections on rims.

- **Inadequate processing time or temperature:**
  Ensure proper boiling in water-bath canning or correct pressure and timing in pressure canning.

Amish advice: If a jar fails to seal, refrigerate promptly and consume within one week, or reprocess within 24 hours using a fresh lid and proper canning procedures.

Problem 2: Loss of Liquid (Siphoning)

Siphoning occurs when liquid escapes jars during processing, resulting in less liquid in the jar once cooled.

Possible Causes and Solutions:

- **Rapid temperature changes:**
  Allow jars to rest in the canner for 5–10 minutes after processing ends before removal, preventing sudden changes in temperature.

- **Incorrect headspace:**
  Follow precise headspace recommendations—usually ¼-inch for jams, ½-inch for pickles, and 1 inch for pressure-canned goods.

- **Fluctuating pressure (pressure canning):**
  Maintain consistent pressure throughout the process, adjusting heat gently to keep it stable.

- **Overfilling jars:**
  Leave proper headspace; tightly packed jars tend to siphon.

Amish practical solution: If minor siphoning occurs and jars remain sealed, contents are usually safe. However, use these jars first, as quality may decline faster.

Problem 3: Floating Fruit or Vegetables

Floating produce is common, though not harmful. It does affect appearance and quality slightly.

Possible Causes and Solutions:

- **Produce packed too loosely:**
  Pack fruits and vegetables firmly (but gently) to minimize floating.

- **Overripe or lightweight produce:**
  Choose firm, fresh, and slightly underripe produce for optimal results.

- **Trapped air bubbles:**
  Always remove air bubbles thoroughly with a bubble remover or spatula before sealing jars.

Amish tip: Turning jars gently every hour during cooling helps redistribute contents evenly.

Problem 4: Cloudy Liquid in Jars

Cloudy liquid typically doesn't compromise safety, but clarity improves appearance and quality.

Possible Causes and Solutions:

- **Hard water minerals:**
  Use filtered, distilled, or softened water in your brines and syrups to ensure clarity.

- **Starch release (especially corn, potatoes):**
  Blanch starchy vegetables briefly before packing jars to reduce cloudiness.

- **Improper processing:**
  Ensure the correct processing time and temperature; over-processing sometimes leads to cloudiness.

Amish wisdom: Slight cloudiness in pickles can indicate fermentation, which may still be safe and tasty. Examine carefully and discard if jars smell off or moldy upon opening.

Problem 5: Mold Formation

Mold is unsafe and requires immediate disposal of the jar's contents.

Possible Causes and Solutions:

- **Incomplete processing or poor seals:**
  Follow exact canning times, use proper sealing techniques, and inspect jars regularly.

- **Insufficient acidity (for water-bath canning):**
  Always use tested recipes and include acid (vinegar, lemon juice) when canning borderline-acid foods like tomatoes.

Amish rule of thumb: Discard any moldy jar contents immediately without tasting. Mold indicates spoilage and potential bacteria.

Problem 6: Darkening or Discoloration of Food

Darkening is usually safe but affects appearance and flavor quality.

Possible Causes and Solutions:

- **Oxidation (fruits, potatoes):**
  Dip cut produce into lemon juice or ascorbic acid solution before packing jars to maintain color.

- **Using iron or copper utensils:**
  Always use stainless steel, glass, or enamelware to prevent discoloration.

- **Extended exposure to heat:**
  Follow exact processing times; excessive heating can darken foods.

Amish practical tip: Slight darkening of canned apples, pears, or potatoes is normal and safe. Only discard if food smells spoiled or moldy when opened.

Problem 7: Jars Breaking During Canning

Broken jars are a disappointing—and avoidable—occurrence.

Possible Causes and Solutions:

- **Cracks or chips unnoticed beforehand:**
  Inspect jars carefully under good lighting before use.

- **Temperature shock:**
  Warm jars slightly before filling; never place hot jars directly onto cold surfaces or vice versa.

- **Improper rack placement:**
  Always use racks in your canner; never allow jars to touch the bottom directly.

Amish wisdom: If a jar breaks during processing, remove it carefully after cooling and inspect your canner carefully for fragments. Remaining jars are safe if seals remain intact.

Practical Amish Solutions at a Glance:

- **Preventive care:**
  Always maintain tools, check jars thoroughly, and handle them gently.

- **Follow tested recipes:**
  Never deviate from trusted sources; recipes are rigorously tested for safety.

- **Routine inspections:**
  Regularly check your pantry for signs of spoilage, mold, or broken seals. Early detection prevents waste and protects health.

These Amish troubleshooting tips, tried and tested over generations, empower you to confidently overcome common canning challenges. Every challenge you overcome brings deeper wisdom, a better understanding of your preserved foods, and the joyful satisfaction of a pantry filled with nutritious, wholesome food for your family.

Storage Advice for Your Canned Foods

In Amish homes, preserving food goes beyond the simple act of filling jars and sealing lids—proper storage is just as crucial. Growing up in an Amish family, I learned early that careful storage ensures your canned goods stay flavorful, nutritious, and safe long into the future. Here, I'll share practical, proven advice that generations of Amish homemakers trust to keep their pantry shelves stocked and preserved foods in optimal condition.

Choosing the Perfect Storage Space

Proper storage begins with selecting the ideal place in your home for your canned goods. Amish households traditionally store canned items in cool, dry, and dark environments—such as cellars, basements, pantries, or dedicated storage rooms.

Ideal Storage Conditions:

- **Temperature:**
  Store jars between 50°F–70°F (10°C–21°C). Constant, cooler temperatures slow spoilage and maintain optimal food quality.

- **Darkness:**
  Keep jars away from direct sunlight or fluorescent lighting, which can discolor food and accelerate nutrient loss.

- **Dryness:**
  Prevent moisture and humidity buildup to avoid rusting bands, mold formation, and damaged labels.

Amish Tip:
If your home lacks a traditional cellar or basement, consider a dedicated cupboard or closet away from heat sources (stoves, radiators, or direct sunlight) to protect your preserved foods.

Organizing Your Pantry the Amish Way

Order and cleanliness ensure the longest shelf life and highest quality of preserved foods. Organize your canned goods thoughtfully:

- **Label clearly:**
  Each jar should have a label indicating contents and preservation date. This allows easy tracking of your inventory and proper rotation.

- **Use the "first in, first out" method:**
  Always consume the oldest jars first to maintain freshness and prevent waste.

- **Separate food categories:**
  Group similar items together, such as jams, pickles, vegetables, meats, fruits, and soups. This helps you quickly locate what you need and easily monitor your supply.

Amish Practical Wisdom:
Keep a simple pantry journal or inventory sheet near your canned goods, noting quantities, preservation dates, and usage, helping you manage your supplies throughout the seasons.

Removing Bands for Storage

Amish tradition advises removing bands after jars are fully cooled (usually after 24 hours) and sealed. Here's why this matters:

- Prevents rust from forming under bands, which can lead to contamination.
- Allows quick visual inspection for unsealed jars or spoilage (bulging lids, leaks, or discoloration).
- Preserves bands in good condition for reuse in future seasons.

Amish Tip:
Store extra bands in airtight bags or containers, away from moisture, for easy reuse in future canning sessions.

Inspecting Your Jars Regularly

Routine checks ensure the safety and quality of your canned goods:

- Regularly examine your jars monthly. Look for signs such as bulging lids, leaks, discoloration, or mold inside jars.
- Never consume food from jars with questionable seals, signs of spoilage, or abnormal appearance. Discard the entire contents immediately.

Amish Wisdom:
When opening jars, always smell and visually inspect contents closely. Spoiled food typically has noticeable odors or unusual textures—trust your senses.

Shelf-Life Recommendations (Amish Guidelines):

- **High-acid foods (jams, pickles, tomatoes, fruits):**
  Ideally consumed within 1–2 years. While they remain safe beyond that, quality, taste, and nutritional value gradually diminish.
- **Low-acid foods (vegetables, meats, soups):**
  Best used within 1–2 years for maximum quality, though safely processed jars can last up to several years when stored properly.

Amish Practical Advice:
Always trust your senses when determining jar freshness. Properly sealed jars can remain safe much longer than standard guidelines, but Amish practice emphasizes cautious judgment.

Handling Opened Jars and Leftovers

Once opened, canned foods need refrigeration:

- Consume refrigerated contents within one week (ideally sooner).
- Transfer unused portions to clean containers with tight-fitting lids before refrigeration, preventing contamination and spoilage.

Amish Practical Tip:
If you frequently don't finish a jar quickly, consider preserving foods in smaller jars (half-pints or pint sizes) to minimize waste.

Common Storage Problems and Solutions

- **Rusty or corroded lids:**
  High humidity typically causes rust. Use a dehumidifier or moisture absorbers in storage areas.
- **Sticky or stained jars:**
  Leaks during canning can cause sticky residue. Clean jars thoroughly before storing to prevent mold and pests.
- **Fading labels or unclear writing:**
  Use permanent markers or waterproof labels to keep details legible.

Amish Storage Checklist at a Glance:

- ✓ Cool (50–70°F), dark, and dry location
- ✓ Clear, dated labels
- ✓ Regular inspections
- ✓ Bands removed after sealing
- ✓ Proper rotation ("first in, first out")

- ✓ Sensible jar sizing to minimize waste

By following these Amish-tested storage principles, your preserved foods will stay safe, delicious, and nutritious, enhancing your pantry with wholesome, homemade goods that sustain your family through every season.

CHAPTER 2: AMISH CURING METHODS FOR MEAT

Choosing and Preparing Meat for Curing

For generations, curing meat has been an essential skill in Amish households, not only preserving meat for winter but providing rich, flavorful meals throughout the year. Growing up Amish, curing meat was a cherished tradition in our family. From selecting quality cuts to carefully preparing the meat for preservation, each step was performed thoughtfully, guided by tradition, practicality, and experience. In this section, I'll share the key Amish practices and advice for choosing and preparing your meat properly for curing.

Choosing the Right Cuts of Meat

Selecting quality cuts of meat is the foundation of successful curing. While almost any cut of pork or beef can be cured, traditional Amish practices focus on specific cuts ideal for curing, based on texture, fat content, and flavor.

Best pork cuts for curing:

- **Ham:** The hind leg is perfect for curing whole hams. Amish-cured ham is traditionally a winter staple, enjoyed at holiday meals and family gatherings.

- **Bacon:** Pork belly, with its rich marbling of fat and meat, is ideal for curing bacon. Amish bacon is known for its sweetness, crispness, and deep flavor.

- **Pork shoulder or Boston butt:** Excellent for cured pork roasts, country hams, and sausages, these cuts offer rich flavor and tenderness when properly cured.

- **Pork loin:** Great for Canadian-style bacon or cured pork chops, this leaner cut cures quickly and has an appealing texture.

Beef cuts best for curing:

- **Brisket:** Amish households traditionally cure brisket to make flavorful corned beef or pastrami, highly prized during winter months.

- **Round or rump roast:** Lean, flavorful, and versatile cuts often cured and sliced thinly for dried beef or chipped beef dishes.

- **Eye of round:** Ideal for dry curing and making traditional Amish dried beef, which lasts for months and serves as a delicious snack or meal ingredient.

Amish Practical Wisdom:
Always select fresh, high-quality cuts from trusted sources—ideally local farms or butchers you know well. Freshness greatly influences the flavor and longevity of your cured meats.

Inspecting and Evaluating Meat Quality

Careful inspection is crucial before beginning the curing process. Follow these guidelines:

- **Color:**
  Meat should appear fresh and vibrant—deep pink to red for pork, rich red for beef. Avoid meat that is grayish, pale, or excessively dark.

- **Fat:**
  Healthy fat should be creamy white or slightly off-white, firm but not hard. Avoid overly yellow or soft, slimy fat.

- **Smell:**
  Fresh meat has a neutral or slightly sweet smell. Any off odors indicate spoilage and should be discarded.

- **Texture:**
  Meat should feel firm and spring back slightly when pressed. Reject cuts that feel slimy, sticky, or excessively wet.

Amish tip:
Always inspect meat carefully, using your senses as your guide. If something seems off, trust your intuition and choose a better cut.

Preparing Meat for Curing (Amish Step-by-Step Approach)

Proper meat preparation ensures thorough curing, safety, and superior flavor. Follow these practical Amish steps:

Step 1: Trimming and Cleaning

- Trim excess fat, but leave a moderate amount to ensure juiciness and flavor.
- Remove any silverskin, tendons, and blood vessels that may toughen during curing.
- Rinse meat gently under cold running water, then pat dry completely with clean towels. Moisture prevents proper curing.

Amish Practical Advice:
Avoid excessive trimming—some fat is essential for flavor and texture. Trim conservatively, leaving a thin fat layer intact.

Step 2: Cutting and Portioning (Optional)

- For whole hams or large cuts, curing is typically done whole.
- For bacon, brisket, or smaller cuts, portion meat into manageable sizes for easier handling and quicker curing.
- Slice uniformly (especially bacon slabs or beef roasts) to ensure even curing throughout the meat.

Amish tip:
For beginners, smaller portions are easier to manage and cure successfully. With experience, you can confidently tackle larger cuts.

Step 3: Chilling the Meat

- Place prepared meat in a cool area or refrigerator for several hours before curing. Chilled meat absorbs curing mixtures better and prevents bacterial growth during early stages.

Important Amish Reminder:
Never cure meat at room temperature—always start with chilled meat to ensure safety.

Amish Guidelines for Safe Meat Handling Before Curing:

- Always sanitize knives, cutting boards, and utensils thoroughly before and after handling raw meat.
- Keep raw meat refrigerated or cool during preparation to maintain freshness.
- Avoid cross-contamination by washing hands regularly, and never handle cooked or ready-to-eat foods simultaneously with raw meat.

Amish Secrets to Enhancing Flavor Before Curing:

- For pork and beef cuts, Amish cooks often score the surface lightly to help curing mixture penetrate deeply.
- Marinate or briefly soak meat in cold water or mild salt brine for 2–3 hours before applying the curing mix—this encourages uniform curing, juiciness, and tenderness.

Amish Wisdom:
Adding spices or herbs directly to the curing mixture enhances flavor significantly. Consider black pepper, brown sugar, garlic, juniper berries, bay leaves, or maple syrup for delicious traditional Amish-style cured meats.

By thoughtfully choosing and preparing meat using these practical Amish guidelines, you're laying the foundation for successfully cured meats that are safe, delicious, and rich in flavor—just as generations of Amish families have perfected over time.

Easy Salt and Sugar Curing Mixtures

In traditional Amish households, curing mixtures are simple, effective, and have stood the test of time. Growing up in an Amish community, I learned that the best recipes for curing meat are those which rely on basic ingredients—primarily salt, sugar, and simple herbs and spices. These straightforward mixtures not only preserve meat safely but also enhance its natural flavor, creating delicious cured meats that Amish families enjoy year-round. In this section, I'll share practical recipes for easy-to-use curing mixtures, along with traditional Amish wisdom to guide you in creating your own perfectly cured meat at home.

Understanding Salt and Sugar in Amish Curing

Before we jump into recipes, it's helpful to understand the role each ingredient plays in the curing process:

- **Salt:** Draws moisture out of the meat, preserving it by preventing harmful bacteria growth. Amish families prefer plain, non-iodized salt or kosher salt for curing, as iodine can affect taste and texture.
- **Sugar:** Balances the saltiness, helps retain moisture and tenderness, and imparts a subtle sweetness. Amish traditionally use brown sugar, white granulated sugar, or even molasses or maple syrup to add depth of flavor.

Traditional Amish Salt and Sugar Curing Mix (All-Purpose)

This versatile mixture is perfect for pork cuts (such as ham, bacon, pork shoulder) or beef cuts (brisket, round roast, eye of round).

Ingredients:

- 2 cups kosher or non-iodized salt
- 1 cup brown sugar (packed tightly)
- 2 tablespoons freshly ground black pepper (optional but recommended for flavor)
- 1 tablespoon ground cloves (optional for pork or holiday hams)
- 1 tablespoon garlic powder (optional, especially nice for beef cuts)

Preparation:

- In a clean bowl, combine all ingredients thoroughly, ensuring even distribution of salt, sugar, and spices.
- Store the mixture in a sealed glass or plastic container in a cool, dry place until ready for use.

Amish Practical Advice:
This mixture is shelf-stable and will last several months stored in airtight conditions. Make it in large batches to save time during curing seasons.

Sweet Maple Sugar Cure (Amish Favorite for Bacon)

This mixture gives bacon a sweet, smoky, Amish-style flavor.

Ingredients:

- 1½ cups kosher or non-iodized salt
- 1½ cups brown sugar
- ½ cup pure maple syrup (Amish traditionally use homemade or locally sourced)
- 2 teaspoons ground black pepper (optional)

Preparation:

- Combine salt and brown sugar thoroughly in a large bowl.
- Drizzle maple syrup over the dry mixture and stir until evenly moist and crumbly.
- Add pepper if desired and mix well again.
- Use this cure immediately, as moisture from maple syrup limits shelf-life.

Amish tip:
For a more intense maple flavor, lightly brush additional maple syrup onto bacon slabs midway through curing.

Amish Quick Cure (Ideal for Small Cuts and Beginners)

Perfect for small pork loins, beef roasts, or chicken breasts intended for shorter curing periods.

Ingredients:

- 1 cup kosher salt or non-iodized salt
- ½ cup white granulated sugar
- 1 teaspoon ground black pepper (optional)
- ½ teaspoon dried rosemary or thyme (optional but flavorful)

Preparation:

- Mix all ingredients thoroughly in a clean bowl until evenly combined.
- Store in an airtight container or use immediately to cure smaller cuts for shorter durations (typically 24–48 hours).

Amish practical wisdom:
The smaller grains of white sugar help this mixture penetrate meat quickly, ideal for speedy curing or when time is limited.

Using Your Curing Mixtures (Amish Step-by-Step Method)

Follow this traditional Amish method for applying your curing mixtures effectively:

1. **Preparation:**
   Clean and pat dry your meat thoroughly. Chilled meat is ideal for curing.

2. **Application:**
   Generously coat meat on all sides, pressing gently to ensure the curing mixture adheres well.
   For thicker cuts (hams, briskets), rub the mixture deeply into any scored areas or cuts.

3. **Curing:**
   Place meat in a non-reactive container (glass, ceramic, food-grade plastic).
   Refrigerate or store in a cool area, turning the meat every 24 hours to ensure even curing.

4. **Duration:**
   Cure pork belly (bacon) for 7–10 days, pork shoulder or ham for 10–14 days, and smaller beef cuts for 5–7 days. Larger cuts may require additional time.

Amish tip:
When curing pork or beef in colder months, Amish families traditionally hang meat in cool basements or outdoor sheds (kept consistently cool around 40°F/4°C).

Amish Practical Tips for Perfect Curing:

- Always use fresh, high-quality salt and sugar for best flavor.
- Adjust the sugar ratio according to your taste preference; a sweeter cure complements bacon, while less sugar suits traditional country ham or beef roasts.
- Be patient—proper curing takes time. Amish tradition values slow, steady curing as the key to flavor and safety.

Customizing Your Amish Curing Mixtures

Traditional Amish families often create signature curing blends by experimenting with flavors. Try adding these spices and herbs to customize your curing:

- **Juniper berries:** Add earthy, traditional flavor (ideal for beef).
- **Bay leaves:** Enhance savory notes, particularly for pork roasts.
- **Garlic and onion powders:** Give robust flavor to beef cuts or sausages.
- **Mustard seeds:** A popular Amish addition for hams and pork shoulders, offering mild tanginess.

By using these practical Amish curing mixtures and following traditional techniques, your meats will become flavorful staples, safely preserved and ready to nourish your family year-round—just as generations of Amish households have enjoyed for centuries.

Step-by-Step Guide to Dry Curing at Home

Dry curing is a traditional Amish preservation method cherished for its simplicity, flavor, and lasting quality. Growing up in an Amish family, I recall watching my father and grandfather meticulously dry-cure meats, creating rich, savory ham, bacon, and beef that sustained our family throughout the seasons. Though dry curing requires patience and care, the reward is a deliciously flavorful preserved meat that embodies the very essence of Amish simplicity. In this practical guide, I'll walk you step-by-step through the traditional Amish method of dry curing meats safely and effectively at home.

Step 1: Choosing and Preparing the Meat

Begin by selecting a suitable meat cut (pork belly for bacon, hind leg for ham, brisket or round roast for beef):

- Select fresh, high-quality meat from a trusted source.
- Trim excess fat but leave a moderate layer intact for flavor.
- Wash meat gently under cool water, then pat completely dry with clean towels.

Amish tip:
Chill your meat for several hours before applying your curing mixture; cold meat absorbs flavors and salts more effectively.

Step 2: Preparing Your Dry Cure

Use one of the traditional Amish curing mixtures provided in the previous section, or create your own custom blend based on taste preferences.

A basic Amish dry cure includes:

- 2 cups kosher salt or non-iodized salt
- 1 cup brown sugar
- 2 tablespoons ground black pepper (optional)

Mix thoroughly, ensuring even distribution. Store mixture dry, and prepare enough to generously coat the meat on all sides.

Step 3: Applying the Cure to Your Meat

Follow this traditional Amish application method carefully for best results:

- Place your meat onto a clean, non-reactive surface (plastic, ceramic, or glass).
- Rub a generous amount of curing mixture onto every surface, pressing firmly and ensuring thorough coverage.

- For thicker cuts (such as ham or brisket), rub deeply into scored or cut areas to enhance absorption.

Amish Practical Wisdom:
Do not skimp on curing mixture—Amish tradition teaches that generous curing is essential for flavor and safety.

Step 4: Storing Meat for Curing

- Transfer your coated meat into a non-reactive container or wrap it tightly in food-grade plastic wrap or muslin cloth.

- Place the meat into a refrigerator or cold cellar (ideally 36–40°F / 2–4°C).

- Elevate or place on racks to allow any released moisture to drain away from meat, preventing spoilage.

Amish Tip:
If wrapping meat, make sure to check regularly for accumulated liquid, draining it carefully as needed.

Step 5: Curing Period and Turning the Meat

- Cure meat consistently, turning daily for even absorption. This ensures the cure penetrates uniformly and prevents spoilage.
- Recommended curing durations (traditional Amish guidelines):
    - **Pork belly (bacon):** Cure 7–10 days.
    - **Whole ham:** Cure 14–21 days (depending on size).
    - **Beef cuts (brisket, round roast):** Cure 7–10 days.
- Each day, inspect meat carefully for uniform curing and remove excess liquid if present.

Step 6: Rinsing and Drying the Cured Meat

After the curing period ends:

- Remove meat from cure and rinse thoroughly under cool running water to remove excess salt and cure residue.
- Pat the meat completely dry with clean, absorbent towels. Ensure it's entirely dry to prevent mold growth.

Amish Wisdom:
For saltier meats (such as traditional country ham), soaking meat briefly (30–60 minutes) in fresh cold water reduces excessive saltiness before drying.

Step 7: Drying and Aging the Meat

This traditional step enhances flavor and preservation further:

- Place the rinsed and dried meat onto clean racks or hang in a cool, dry, and well-ventilated area (ideally 50–60°F / 10–16°C).

- Allow meat to air-dry and age naturally for approximately 1–3 weeks, depending on size and desired texture.

- During aging, the meat's exterior dries further, creating a protective layer that enhances preservation and flavor.

Amish Practical Tip:
Use muslin cloth or cheesecloth to loosely cover the meat during aging, protecting it from dust and insects while allowing proper airflow.

Step 8: Checking for Properly Cured Meat (Traditional Amish Method)

Properly dry-cured meat should feel firm yet slightly yielding when pressed:

- Check the color: Properly cured pork or beef will have deep, rich colors (dark pink to red), not pale or overly dark.
- Smell carefully: Properly cured meat smells pleasantly cured, slightly sweet and savory. Any sour or off odors indicate spoilage—discard immediately.

Step 9: Final Storage of Dry-Cured Meats

Once fully cured and dried:

- Wrap meat in clean muslin cloth or parchment paper for long-term storage.
- Store meat in cool, dry, dark areas (ideally 50–60°F / 10–16°C), typically in a pantry, cellar, or basement.
- Properly dry-cured meats stored traditionally can safely last for months.

Amish Wisdom:
In humid conditions, Amish families traditionally coat cured meats with lard, beeswax, or even black pepper to protect from moisture and pests, extending shelf life significantly.

Amish Tips to Enhance Your Dry Curing:

- Adjust spices and herbs in your curing mixtures to match your personal taste.
- Experiment carefully, keeping track of recipes in a simple curing journal to repeat your successes easily.
- Consider smoking your cured meats after initial curing for added flavor, preservation, and authenticity.

By following this step-by-step traditional Amish method, you'll master dry curing at home, confidently producing flavorful, wholesome preserved meats that sustain and delight your family throughout every season.

Common Mistakes and How to Avoid Them

Throughout generations, Amish households have perfected meat-curing techniques by learning from experience, often through trial and error. Growing up Amish, I saw firsthand that mistakes happen, but what truly matters is learning from them. In this section, I'll share practical insights into common mistakes made during meat curing, along with clear, time-tested Amish solutions to ensure your cured meats turn out perfectly every time.

Mistake 1: Using the Wrong Type of Salt

Problem:
Using iodized salt or fine-grained table salt can result in a bitter flavor, inconsistent curing, or poor preservation.

Amish Solution:
Always choose coarse kosher salt, non-iodized pickling salt, or sea salt. Coarse grains absorb evenly, ensuring thorough curing without altering the meat's taste.

Mistake 2: Insufficient Curing Time

Problem:
Removing meat from the cure too early can leave it under-cured, increasing spoilage risk and compromising flavor and texture.

Amish Solution:
Follow recommended curing durations precisely:

- Bacon or pork belly: 7–10 days
- Ham (large cuts): 14–21 days
- Beef cuts: 7–10 days

When in doubt, Amish wisdom advises allowing additional curing time to guarantee safety and flavor development.

Mistake 3: Overly Salty Meat

Problem:
Excessively salty cured meats often result from too much curing mixture, insufficient rinsing, or not soaking salty cuts after curing.

Amish Solution:
Carefully measure your curing mixtures to maintain proper proportions (typically 2:1 salt-to-sugar ratio). After curing, rinse meat thoroughly, and for extra salty cuts (like country ham), soak meat in cold water for 30–60 minutes before drying.

Mistake 4: Inconsistent Curing Mixture Application

Problem:
Applying curing mixture unevenly causes inconsistent curing, leading to spoilage spots, uneven texture, or unbalanced flavors.

Amish Solution:
Rub your curing mixture generously and uniformly onto every surface of the meat. Regularly turn and inspect meat daily, ensuring the cure penetrates uniformly.

Mistake 5: Poor Temperature Control During Curing

Problem:
Curing meat at too high or fluctuating temperatures promotes bacterial growth, spoilage, and potential health risks.

Amish Solution:
Maintain meat temperatures consistently between 36–40°F (2–4°C). Amish households traditionally cure meat in cold cellars, basements, or refrigerators set at these temperatures, ensuring consistent safety and quality.

Mistake 6: Improper Drying and Aging

Problem:
Rushing drying and aging, or drying in unsuitable conditions, leads to mold growth, spoilage, or poor flavor.

Amish Solution:
After curing, dry meat properly:

- Rinse thoroughly and pat completely dry.
- Dry meat in cool (50–60°F / 10–16°C), dark, well-ventilated places.
- Use cheesecloth or muslin cloth to protect from dust and pests while allowing air circulation.

Check meat regularly during drying, removing any mold immediately using vinegar and water solution if mild mold occurs.

Mistake 7: Neglecting Cleanliness and Sanitation

Problem:
Cross-contamination or inadequate cleanliness causes spoilage or dangerous bacterial growth.

Amish Solution:
Always sanitize tools, cutting boards, containers, and hands thoroughly before and after handling meat. Amish tradition emphasizes cleanliness as essential for successful curing and safe preservation.

Mistake 8: Choosing Low-Quality or Old Meat

Problem:
Poor-quality meat or meat that's past its prime can't be safely or effectively cured, risking spoilage and inferior taste.

Amish Solution:
Select fresh, high-quality cuts from trusted sources. Inspect meat closely for color, smell, and texture, choosing cuts that are fresh and wholesome.

Mistake 9: Not Labeling or Documenting Properly

Problem:
Forgetting when meat was cured or what mixture was used leads to confusion, uncertain safety, and difficulty in repeating successful results.

Amish Solution:
Label every cut clearly with curing dates, mixture details, and meat type. Maintain a simple curing journal to easily track results, adjustments, and successes, simplifying future curing projects.

Amish Quick Checklist to Avoid Curing Mistakes:

- ✓ Use only coarse, non-iodized salt.
- ✓ Maintain consistent, cool temperatures throughout curing.
- ✓ Follow exact curing durations.
- ✓ Apply curing mixtures evenly and generously.
- ✓ Rinse and dry thoroughly before aging.
- ✓ Store dried meat properly in cool, dry conditions.
- ✓ Always practice meticulous cleanliness.
- ✓ Clearly label and document each curing project.

Learning from these common mistakes, armed with practical Amish solutions, you'll quickly master the art of curing meats. With each batch, your skills improve, allowing you to enjoy delicious, safely preserved meats prepared the traditional Amish way—flavorful, nourishing, and enjoyed across generations.

Practical Storage Tips for Cured Meats

In Amish households, properly storing cured meats is just as essential as the curing process itself. Growing up Amish, I learned that careful, mindful storage ensures cured meats remain safe, flavorful, and enjoyable throughout the year. The techniques shared here, refined through generations of Amish experience, will help you keep your carefully cured meats fresh, delicious, and safe for your family to enjoy for months or even years.

Choosing Your Storage Environment

A cool, dry, dark storage area is essential to maintaining the quality and safety of your cured meats. Amish families traditionally utilize spaces like cellars, basements, or dedicated meat storage rooms.

Ideal conditions for storing cured meats:

- **Temperature:** Maintain temperatures between 50°F and 60°F (10°C–16°C). Cooler, stable temperatures preserve meat texture, flavor, and safety.
- **Humidity:** Low to moderate humidity (50–65%) is optimal. Excess humidity can cause mold, while too little humidity leads to overly dry, tough meat.
- **Darkness:** Protect meats from direct sunlight and artificial lighting, as exposure can accelerate fat rancidity and flavor deterioration.

Amish tip:
If your home lacks a cellar or basement, consider creating a dedicated pantry cupboard or closet away from heat sources and moisture. Use moisture absorbers or a small fan for improved ventilation.

Wrapping and Protecting Cured Meats

Proper wrapping is crucial for long-term storage, as it prevents spoilage, pests, and contamination.

Traditional Amish methods include:

- **Muslin or cheesecloth wrapping:**
  Wrap cured meat tightly in muslin or cheesecloth, allowing the meat

to breathe naturally while preventing contamination and pests. This method is ideal for dry-cured hams, bacon, and beef.

- **Paper wrapping (parchment or butcher paper):**
  Paper wrapping is breathable yet provides protection from dust and insects. Wrap meats snugly in parchment or butcher paper, taping edges securely.

- **Vacuum sealing (modern Amish adaptation):**
  Although less traditional, vacuum sealing preserves freshness exceptionally well, preventing oxidation and mold growth, making it suitable for smaller cuts or slices.

Amish Wisdom:
For very long-term storage, Amish households sometimes coat cured meats lightly in lard or beeswax, creating a natural protective barrier against moisture, pests, and mold.

Hanging and Airflow (Traditional Amish Method)

Proper airflow significantly extends the shelf life of cured meats:

- Hang wrapped meats from sturdy hooks or racks in cool, ventilated areas. This keeps them off surfaces and allows consistent air circulation, preventing mold growth and moisture accumulation.

- Leave adequate space between individual pieces of meat to maximize airflow and reduce the risk of spoilage.

Amish practical tip:
Regularly inspect hanging meats, adjusting spacing or rearranging to maintain optimal airflow conditions.

Regular Inspections for Quality and Safety

Frequent inspections help ensure safety, freshness, and taste:

- Check meats every few weeks for signs of mold, moisture buildup, or pests.

- Small, harmless white molds are occasionally common on dry-cured meats. Amish households traditionally wipe this away gently using a vinegar-and-water-soaked cloth.

- Discard meats immediately if you notice dark or black mold, slimy textures, or off-putting odors, as these indicate spoilage or harmful bacterial growth.

Amish safety rule:
Always trust your senses—when meat appears or smells spoiled, err on the side of caution and discard it promptly.

Slicing and Short-term Storage (After Opening)

Once a cured meat is sliced or opened:

- Wrap the remaining piece securely in wax paper, parchment, or muslin cloth, then store refrigerated (below 40°F/4°C).
- For optimal freshness, consume refrigerated cured meats within two weeks after opening.

Amish tip:
To prolong freshness, slice only the amount needed at one time, keeping the remaining cured meat whole until ready for use.

Freezing Cured Meats (Amish Practical Advice)

Though less traditional, freezing is a reliable method for extending storage:

- Wrap meats carefully in freezer-safe paper, vacuum-seal, or place them in freezer bags with air removed.
- Label clearly with the freezing date and type of meat. Consume frozen cured meats within 6–12 months for best quality.

Amish wisdom:
Freezing slightly alters meat texture, but flavor remains excellent. To use, thaw slowly in the refrigerator, allowing flavor and texture to remain intact.

Storage Duration Guidelines (Traditional Amish Recommendations):

- **Dry-cured ham:** 6–12 months or longer when properly stored in cool, dry conditions.

- **Dry-cured bacon:** 3–6 months safely stored in cool, dry environments.
- **Dry-cured beef:** 6–9 months when properly wrapped, hung, and ventilated.

(These durations assume optimal Amish storage conditions.)

Amish Storage Checklist at a Glance:

- ✓ Cool (50–60°F), dry, and dark storage area
- ✓ Properly wrapped or coated meats for protection
- ✓ Adequate airflow and hanging storage when possible
- ✓ Regular inspections for mold, pests, and spoilage
- ✓ Clearly labeled packages and rotation system ("first in, first out")

By following these practical Amish storage methods, you can confidently keep your cured meats flavorful, safe, and nutritious, extending the joy and satisfaction of your careful curing efforts throughout the year.

CHAPTER 3: AMISH SMOKING ESSENTIALS

Building a Simple Amish-Style Smokehouse

In Amish communities, smoking meats and cheeses has long been a cornerstone of food preservation, adding rich flavor and ensuring food safety. Growing up Amish, our family's smokehouse was modest yet highly effective—built simply, using materials found close to home, and used year after year to preserve food naturally. In this practical guide, I'll help you construct your own Amish-style smokehouse, sharing traditional methods and insights to create a sturdy, efficient structure that will serve your family for generations.

Why Choose an Amish-Style Smokehouse?

An Amish smokehouse is traditionally built to be simple, durable, and easy to maintain, making it ideal for beginners or anyone who appreciates practicality. Unlike complex commercial smokers, an Amish smokehouse emphasizes straightforward construction, reliability, and simplicity—perfect for safely smoking meat, fish, poultry, and cheese with minimal fuss.

Materials You'll Need (Traditional Amish Recommendations):

Amish smokehouses are traditionally built using affordable, locally-sourced, and durable materials:

- Untreated hardwood lumber (oak, maple, cedar, or hickory planks)
- Fire-resistant bricks (for the firebox or base)
- Metal hinges and latch for the door
- Stainless steel or cast-iron grates and hooks for hanging
- Galvanized or stainless-steel chimney pipe (optional but recommended)
- Corrugated metal, shingles, or wood planks for roofing
- Concrete blocks or bricks for the foundation (optional but recommended)
- Nails, screws, and basic hand tools (saw, hammer, drill, screwdriver, level)

Amish tip:
Avoid treated lumber, paint, or chemical sealants—they release toxins during smoking. Use natural, untreated hardwood for the safest, best-tasting smoked food.

Step-by-Step Construction of Your Amish Smokehouse:

Step 1: Choosing Your Location

- Select a location at least 15–20 feet away from other buildings for safety and smoke management.
- Ensure good airflow around the smokehouse; slight elevation or gentle slope helps ensure natural ventilation.

Step 2: Laying the Foundation

- Build a solid foundation from concrete blocks or bricks measuring approximately 4 feet wide by 4 feet deep. A stable foundation improves smokehouse durability and ensures safety.

- Level the foundation carefully using a carpenter's level.

Step 3: Constructing the Floor

- Lay down untreated hardwood planks or fire-resistant bricks atop your foundation. Bricks retain heat better and improve fire safety.

- For traditional Amish setups, leaving gaps between floorboards or bricks improves airflow and smoke circulation.

Step 4: Building the Frame

- Using untreated hardwood lumber, build the vertical frame, typically 6–8 feet tall, with dimensions around 4 feet wide by 4 feet deep.
- Securely fasten vertical corner posts using sturdy screws or nails to ensure stability.
- Connect corner posts with horizontal lumber pieces at the top, middle, and bottom for strength.

Step 5: Adding the Walls

- Nail or screw hardwood planks onto the frame securely, ensuring they fit tightly together but leaving slight natural gaps (about ¼-inch) for airflow.
- Amish families traditionally prefer vertical plank construction for improved structural integrity and smoke circulation.

Step 6: Constructing the Door

- Frame out a sturdy, hinged door large enough for easy access—usually around 2 feet wide by 5 feet tall.

- Attach durable metal hinges and latch securely, ensuring a snug fit to prevent smoke escape.

- Amish tradition often includes a small sliding wooden vent near the bottom and top of the door for adjustable airflow.

Step 7: Building the Roof

- Attach rafters at a slight angle or pitched design for easy rainwater runoff.

- Cover rafters with metal sheeting, shingles, or tightly fitted hardwood planks.

- Consider extending the roof slightly beyond walls to protect from rain and weather.

Step 8: Installing Racks and Hooks

- Inside the smokehouse, securely install metal or wooden rods, hooks, and racks at varying heights to accommodate hanging meat, fish, or cheese.

- Amish households traditionally use iron hooks or stainless-steel rods, both durable and easy to clean.

Step 9: Adding a Chimney or Vent Pipe (Optional but Recommended)

- A small chimney pipe installed at the roof's peak enhances airflow and improves smoke control. Amish households often add dampers or adjustable covers to control ventilation.

- Ensure chimney pipe is made from galvanized steel, stainless steel, or fire-resistant material.

Step 10: Building a Simple Firebox (Amish Traditional Method)

- Construct a simple brick firebox inside or just outside the smokehouse to safely burn hardwood and generate smoke.
- Position firebox slightly below floor-level or outside, connected via a small opening or tunnel to channel smoke inside.
- Amish practical tip: Build firebox slightly lower than meat racks to allow smoke to rise naturally, evenly distributing throughout the smokehouse.

Amish Smokehouse Safety Checklist:

- ✓ Maintain safe distances from homes and flammable structures.
- ✓ Use only untreated, chemical-free materials.
- ✓ Secure doors, hinges, and latches firmly.
- ✓ Regularly inspect smokehouse structure and replace damaged wood promptly.
- ✓ Monitor firebox and smoke carefully during operation, never leaving unattended for long periods.

Amish Tips to Enhance Your Smokehouse:

- For improved airflow, Amish smokehouses traditionally include small adjustable vents, which can be opened or closed depending on weather conditions.
- Keep extra bricks or stones handy to adjust airflow or dampen fire intensity during smoking sessions.
- Regularly clean ashes and debris from your firebox, ensuring consistent heat and safe operation.

By following these straightforward Amish steps, you'll construct a practical, efficient, and durable smokehouse ready to produce delicious smoked meats, cheeses, and fish. Like Amish families have for generations, you'll cherish the flavorful rewards of your home-built smokehouse, preserving tradition and enjoying the fruits of your labor season after season.

Selecting the Right Wood for Best Flavor

In Amish households, smoking food isn't just about preservation—it's a cherished tradition deeply rooted in flavor. The type of wood you choose for smoking directly influences the taste, color, and aroma of your meats, fish, and cheeses. Growing up Amish, I learned firsthand how selecting the right wood enhances every bite, turning ordinary foods into something extraordinary. Here, I'll share practical Amish advice and traditional wisdom on choosing wood that perfectly complements and enhances the natural flavors of your smoked goods.

Understanding Wood Selection for Smoking

The type of wood you use directly shapes your food's flavor profile. Amish families traditionally rely on hardwoods, known for clean burning, pleasant aromas, and deep, smoky flavors. Always avoid softwoods (pine, spruce, cedar, fir), as they contain resins that can produce bitter or toxic smoke.

Amish-Preferred Hardwoods and Their Flavors:

Below are traditional Amish favorites, along with guidance on pairing them effectively with different types of food:

1. Hickory (Traditional Amish Favorite):

- **Flavor:** Strong, rich, hearty smoke flavor, with slight sweetness.
- **Ideal for:** Pork (especially bacon, ham), beef brisket, ribs, poultry, cheeses (cheddar, gouda).
- **Amish tip:** Hickory is strong—use sparingly at first until you find the intensity you prefer.

2. Apple Wood:

- **Flavor:** Mild, sweet, fruity, subtly aromatic.
- **Ideal for:** Pork (especially ribs, ham), poultry, fish (trout, salmon), cheeses (mild cheddar, mozzarella).
- **Amish Wisdom:** Apple wood adds gentle sweetness, particularly loved for smoking ham or sausages.

3. Cherry Wood:

- **Flavor:** Sweet, mild, fruity, adds attractive dark reddish-brown color to meats.
- **Ideal for:** Chicken, turkey, pork ribs, ham, duck, salmon.
- **Amish tip:** Cherry blends beautifully with stronger woods like hickory for balanced flavor and appealing color.

4. Maple Wood:

- **Flavor:** Subtly sweet, gentle, mild smoke; produces golden-brown coloring.
- **Ideal for:** Poultry, pork, bacon, vegetables, cheeses (especially Swiss or mild cheddar).
- **Amish advice:** Maple is ideal for beginners—delicate enough to avoid overpowering foods.

5. Oak Wood:

- **Flavor:** Medium to strong flavor, earthy, versatile.
- **Ideal for:** Beef brisket, ribs, pork roasts, wild game, sausages.
- **Amish practical tip:** Oak blends well with sweeter woods (like apple or cherry) for deeper, balanced flavors.

6. Pecan Wood (Less common, yet Amish-appreciated):

- **Flavor:** Medium intensity, nutty, rich, slightly sweet.
- **Ideal for:** Poultry, pork chops, ribs, fish, cheeses.
- **Amish insight:** Pecan is perfect when you want hickory-like flavor but milder intensity.

7. Alder Wood (Traditional for Fish Smoking):

- **Flavor:** Very mild, sweet, clean smoke.
- **Ideal for:** Fish (especially salmon, trout), poultry, mild cheeses.
- **Amish wisdom:** Alder is the traditional Amish choice for delicately flavored smoked fish.

Wood Forms—Choosing Practicality and Convenience:

Traditional Amish smoking uses wood in several practical forms:

- **Logs or Large Chunks:**
  Ideal for smokehouses with separate fireboxes, providing steady, slow-burning smoke suitable for long smoking sessions.

- **Wood Chips or Small Chunks:**
  Convenient, quick to ignite, suitable for shorter smoking periods (poultry, fish, cheeses). Amish households often soak chips briefly (20–30 minutes) in water to produce gentle smoke.

- **Sawdust or Fine Chips:**
  Ideal for cold-smoking (cheeses, cured meats, fish). Burns gently, releasing consistent smoke without excessive heat.

Amish tip:
Always ensure wood is properly dried (seasoned) and untreated—fresh or damp wood can produce undesirable smoke flavors.

Amish Tips for Blending Woods:

Blending wood types creates unique flavors that Amish families appreciate:

- **Hickory + Apple:** Perfect for pork, ribs, bacon, adding balanced sweetness and hearty smoke.

- **Cherry + Oak:** Excellent for beef brisket, pork roasts, offering rich color and full-bodied flavor.

- **Maple + Pecan:** Ideal for poultry, ham, cheese—creates mild, balanced smoke flavor with subtle sweetness.

Experiment thoughtfully, keeping notes to replicate favorite combinations.

Woods to Avoid (Amish Safety Advice):

Amish tradition emphasizes avoiding certain woods due to safety and taste concerns:

- **Softwoods (pine, fir, spruce, cedar):** Produce resinous, bitter smoke unsafe for consumption.

- **Chemically-treated or painted wood:** Releases toxic chemicals—never suitable for food smoking.
- **Rotten, moldy, or damp wood:** Yields bitter, unpleasant smoke flavors and potential toxins.

Always source clean, dry, untreated hardwood from trusted sources.

Storing Your Smoking Wood Properly:

Proper wood storage ensures consistent, high-quality smoke flavor:

- Store wood in a dry, ventilated area, protected from rain, moisture, and pests.
- Season wood properly—air dry outdoors for 6–12 months before use for optimal flavor.
- Keep wood off the ground (on pallets or racks), allowing airflow and preventing mold.

Amish Checklist for Selecting and Using Smoking Woods:

- ✓ Choose suitable hardwood types based on desired flavor.
- ✓ Match wood intensity with food type—delicate wood for fish and cheese, stronger wood for beef and pork.
- ✓ Blend wood types carefully for custom flavors.
- ✓ Avoid softwoods and chemically-treated materials.
- ✓ Properly dry and store wood before use.

By following these practical, traditional Amish guidelines for selecting smoking wood, you'll enhance your food with exceptional, authentic flavors. Just like Amish families have done for generations, you'll discover the joy and satisfaction of crafting uniquely smoked foods, richly flavored by nature and tradition.

Hot Smoking vs. Cold Smoking: A Practical Guide

In Amish tradition, smoking food is both an art and a skill passed down through generations. Understanding the differences between **hot smoking** and **cold smoking** is essential for achieving the best flavor, texture, and safety for your smoked foods. Growing up Amish, I learned the practical wisdom behind each method, discovering how and when to apply these smoking techniques to create delicious, safe, and well-preserved meals. Here, I'll guide you through the practicalities of hot and cold smoking, sharing traditional Amish insights that will enable you to master both methods confidently.

Hot Smoking: Traditional Amish Method for Cooking and Preserving

Hot smoking cooks food gently and infuses it with smoky flavor simultaneously. This method is perfect for meats, poultry, fish, and even vegetables, creating tender, flavorful dishes ideal for immediate consumption or short-term storage.

Typical Temperature: 165°F–250°F (74°C–121°C)
Cooking Time: Generally 1–6 hours, depending on food size and type.

Foods Best Suited for Hot Smoking:

- Pork (ham, bacon, ribs, sausages)
- Beef (brisket, ribs, roast cuts)
- Poultry (whole chicken, turkey, duck)
- Fish (trout, salmon, catfish)
- Vegetables (peppers, potatoes, corn)

Amish Practical Step-by-Step Guide to Hot Smoking:

1. **Preparing Your Meat or Food:**
    - Brine, cure, or season your food before smoking. Brining adds moisture; curing enhances flavor and preservation.
2. **Setting Up Your Smoker:**
    - Light your wood or charcoal, ensuring stable temperatures between 165°F and 250°F (74°C–121°C).

- Amish families traditionally use hardwoods like hickory, oak, apple, or maple for hot smoking.

3. **Hot Smoking Process:**
    - Place food directly onto smoker racks or hooks.
    - Maintain steady temperatures throughout the smoking period, periodically adding wood chunks or chips as necessary.

4. **Monitoring Internal Temperatures:**
    - Regularly check the internal temperature of meats using a reliable food thermometer to ensure safe cooking.
    - Common Amish-safe internal cooking temperatures:
        - Poultry: 165°F (74°C)
        - Pork and Beef: 145°F–160°F (63°C–71°C)
        - Fish: 145°F (63°C)

5. **Resting and Storing:**
    - After hot smoking, allow meats to rest 10–15 minutes before slicing, enhancing tenderness and flavor.
    - Refrigerate hot-smoked foods promptly and consume within one week, or freeze for extended storage.

Amish Tip:
Hot smoking is especially effective for foods you plan to eat soon after smoking. It cooks and flavors simultaneously, making it convenient for family meals or gatherings.

Cold Smoking: Amish Tradition for Flavor and Long-Term Preservation

Cold smoking is a gentle process of adding flavor without cooking the food fully. Amish families use this technique traditionally to preserve meats, cheeses, and fish, imparting delicious flavors suitable for long-term storage.

Typical Temperature: Below 90°F (32°C) (ideally 60°F–80°F / 15°C–26°C)
Smoking Time: Typically several hours up to several days, depending on flavor intensity and preservation needs.

Foods Best Suited for Cold Smoking:

- Cheeses (cheddar, gouda, Swiss)
- Fish (salmon, trout, herring)
- Cured meats (bacon, ham, salami, sausages)
- Nuts, seeds, salts, spices (for flavoring purposes)

Amish Practical Step-by-Step Guide to Cold Smoking:

1. **Proper Preparation (Critical Step):**
   - Cold-smoked foods must be thoroughly cured or brined first to ensure safety. This step prevents harmful bacterial growth during smoking.
   - Dry-curing or salt-curing meats is a traditional Amish practice before cold smoking.

2. **Creating Smoke Without Heat:**
   - Keep fire away from food by building a separate, small firebox or using a specialized smoke generator, allowing smoke to cool before reaching food.
   - Use hardwood sawdust, fine chips, or pellets, which smolder slowly and produce consistent, gentle smoke.

3. **Cold Smoking Process:**
   - Hang or place food inside your smoke chamber, ensuring it receives gentle, consistent smoke at low temperatures.
   - Smoking typically ranges from 6–12 hours for cheese and small items to 24–48 hours or more for meats like bacon or ham.

4. **Temperature Control:**
   - Closely monitor chamber temperatures to remain consistently below 90°F (32°C). Amish households traditionally cold-smoke during cooler months (late fall, winter, or early spring) to maintain ideal temperatures naturally.

5. **Aging and Storage After Cold Smoking:**
    - After smoking, air-dry or age foods briefly in cool, well-ventilated conditions before refrigeration or storage.
    - Cold-smoked foods like meats and fish require refrigeration, freezing, or continued drying for safe long-term storage.

Amish Safety Advice:
Cold smoking doesn't cook foods fully, making thorough pre-curing and proper storage essential for safety.

Comparing Hot and Cold Smoking: Amish Quick Reference:

Aspect	Hot Smoking	Cold Smoking
Temperature Range	165°F–250°F (74°C–121°C)	Below 90°F (32°C), ideally 60°F–80°F (15°C–26°C)
Time Required	Shorter (1–6 hours typically)	Longer (6 hours to several days)
Food Safety	Cooks food fully; safe for immediate use	Doesn't cook food fully; requires curing beforehand
Foods Typically Smoked	Pork, beef, poultry, fish, vegetables	Cheeses, cured meats, fish, nuts, spices
Primary Purpose	Cooking and flavoring	Flavoring and long-term preservation

Amish Practical Tips for Successful Smoking:
- Always ensure accurate temperature monitoring for safe, delicious results.
- Begin with short smoking times and gradually increase to achieve your desired flavor intensity.

- Maintain good airflow and ventilation in your smokehouse for consistent, even smoke distribution.
- Carefully label smoked foods with dates and methods (hot or cold smoked) for easy identification and proper storage.

By clearly understanding and practicing these traditional Amish methods for hot and cold smoking, you'll master the art of safely and deliciously smoking food at home. Both methods offer unique advantages and flavor profiles, allowing you to preserve and savor wholesome foods just as Amish families have for generations—safely, simply, and flavorfully.

Smoking Meat, Fish, and Cheese Successfully

In Amish tradition, smoking is much more than a preservation method—it's a way to elevate simple foods into deeply flavorful and satisfying meals. From tender smoked ham to richly flavored salmon and delicately smoked cheeses, mastering this skill is both practical and rewarding. As someone who grew up Amish, I've spent countless hours tending the smokehouse, learning exactly what it takes to successfully smoke meat, fish, and cheese. Here, I'll share clear, practical instructions and authentic Amish secrets that will help you achieve consistently delicious results.

Smoking Meat Successfully (Amish Practical Steps)

Best Meats for Smoking:

- Pork (ham, bacon, ribs, shoulder)

- Beef (brisket, ribs, roasts)
- Poultry (chicken, turkey, duck)

Amish Step-by-Step Method:

1. Preparation and Brining:

- Brine meat for 12–24 hours to enhance tenderness and flavor (optional but strongly recommended).
- Rinse meat briefly, then pat dry before placing in the smoker.

Amish tip: Add brown sugar, herbs (sage, rosemary), or spices (pepper, garlic) to brines for deeper flavor.

2. Selecting Wood:

- Hickory, apple, cherry, or maple woods are traditional favorites.
- Hickory pairs beautifully with pork, apple wood enhances poultry, and oak or cherry adds depth to beef.

3. Smoking Process (Hot Smoking):

- Smoke meats at temperatures between 200°F–225°F (93°C–107°C).
- Smoking times vary:
    - Pork shoulder: 6–12 hours
    - Pork ribs: 4–6 hours
    - Whole chicken: 3–4 hours
    - Beef brisket: 8–12 hours
- Maintain consistent temperatures, monitoring closely to avoid overheating.

4. Checking Meat Doneness:

- Use a food thermometer to check internal temperature regularly.
- Ideal Amish-recommended temperatures:
    - Pork: 145°F–165°F (63°C–74°C)
    - Beef: 145°F–160°F (63°C–71°C)

- Poultry: 165°F (74°C)

5. Resting and Storing:

- Allow meat to rest for 10–20 minutes after smoking before slicing.
- Refrigerate promptly if not consumed immediately, or freeze for extended storage.

Smoking Fish Successfully (Traditional Amish Method)

Best Fish for Smoking:

- Salmon, trout, catfish, whitefish, and herring are popular Amish choices.

Amish Step-by-Step Method:

1. Preparation and Brining:

- Brine fish in a salt-sugar solution for 4–8 hours to enhance flavor and moisture retention.
- Rinse thoroughly and air-dry for 1–2 hours until surface forms a slightly tacky film ("pellicle"), essential for smoke adherence.

Amish tip: Add maple syrup or brown sugar to your fish brine for a pleasant sweetness and attractive color.

2. Selecting Wood:

- Alder, apple, cherry, or maple woods offer gentle, sweet smoke flavors ideal for fish.
- Alder is traditionally favored by Amish families for salmon and trout.

3. Smoking Process (Hot or Cold Smoking):

- **Hot Smoking:** Smoke at 175°F–200°F (79°C–93°C) for approximately 2–4 hours until fish reaches 145°F (63°C).
- **Cold Smoking:** Smoke at temperatures below 90°F (32°C) for 12–24 hours. (Fish must be thoroughly cured before cold smoking.)

4. Checking Doneness and Texture:

- Properly smoked fish should flake easily yet retain moisture and firmness.
- Check internal temperature regularly, and visually inspect fish for even coloring and texture.

5. Cooling and Storing:

- Allow fish to cool completely, refrigerate promptly, and consume within one week.
- Amish practical advice: vacuum-seal and freeze smoked fish for longer storage (up to six months).

Smoking Cheese Successfully (Amish Traditional Method)

Best Cheeses for Smoking:

- Cheddar, Gouda, mozzarella, Swiss, provolone, and pepper jack.

Amish Step-by-Step Method (Cold Smoking):

1. Cheese Preparation:

- Cut cheese into uniform blocks or thick slices for even smoke absorption.
- Allow cheese to reach room temperature briefly (30–60 minutes) before smoking.

2. Selecting Wood:

- Apple, cherry, maple, or pecan woods offer delicate, mild flavors ideal for cheese.
- Amish wisdom suggests blending apple and cherry wood for exceptional results.

3. Smoking Process (Cold Smoking Only):

- Maintain smoke temperatures strictly below 90°F (32°C)—ideal is around 70°F (21°C).
- Smoke cheese for 2–6 hours, checking regularly for flavor intensity. Longer smoking provides stronger flavors.

Amish tip: Keep cheese at cooler temperatures by cold-smoking in early mornings or evenings, especially during warmer months.

4. Post-Smoking Storage and Aging:

- Wrap smoked cheese tightly in parchment or wax paper, then refrigerate for 2–4 weeks to allow flavors to mellow and deepen.
- Amish tradition emphasizes aging smoked cheese to improve flavor and texture significantly.

5. Serving and Enjoying:

- Smoked cheese is perfect sliced with bread, crackers, fruit, or incorporated into Amish recipes for added depth and richness.

Amish Quick Reference Guide (Recommended Temperatures and Times):

Food Type	Temperature	Smoking Time
Pork Shoulder	200–225°F (93–107°C)	6–12 hours
Pork Ribs	200–225°F (93–107°C)	4–6 hours
Whole Chicken	200–225°F (93–107°C)	3–4 hours
Beef Brisket	200–225°F (93–107°C)	8–12 hours
Salmon/Trout	Hot: 175–200°F (79–93°C); Cold: <90°F (32°C)	Hot: 2–4 hours; Cold: 12–24 hours
Cheese	Cold: <90°F (32°C)	2–6 hours

Amish Practical Smoking Tips:

- Start smoking at lower temperatures and gradually increase for maximum tenderness and flavor.
- Keep smoker doors closed as much as possible to maintain steady temperatures and smoke concentration.

- Always monitor internal food temperatures closely for safety and perfect doneness.
- Experiment thoughtfully, keeping notes of methods and results to consistently replicate your favorites.

By following these clear, practical Amish guidelines, you'll master the rewarding tradition of smoking meats, fish, and cheeses. Each successful batch of smoked foods will nourish your family, connect you to traditional Amish heritage, and bring the deep satisfaction that comes from creating wholesome, delicious foods preserved through time-tested techniques.

Tips to Perfect Your Smoking Techniques

In Amish communities, the art of smoking food is learned gradually, perfected over generations through patience, practice, and attention to detail. Growing up Amish, I watched elders meticulously tending their smokehouses, sharing invaluable advice that transformed good smoked food into unforgettable meals. Here, I'll pass on the best practical Amish tips and traditional wisdom I've learned to help you perfect your smoking techniques, ensuring consistently delicious, flavorful, and safe results.

Tip 1: Master Temperature Control

Accurate and stable temperature control is the heart of successful smoking. Whether hot or cold smoking, maintaining consistent temperatures ensures food safety, proper texture, and balanced smoke flavor.

- **Amish Practical Advice:**
  Invest in a reliable smoker thermometer or use multiple thermometers placed at different heights to accurately gauge heat distribution.
- **Hot smoking:** Maintain steady temperatures of 200–225°F (93–107°C) throughout the smoking process.
- **Cold smoking:** Keep temperatures consistently below 90°F (32°C), ideally around 70°F (21°C).

Tip 2: Choose High-Quality, Dry Wood

The wood you select profoundly affects flavor and smoke quality:

- Always use clean, dry (seasoned), untreated hardwood.
- Avoid damp, moldy, resinous, or chemically-treated woods, which can produce bitter, unsafe smoke.

Amish tip:
Season your hardwood outdoors for 6–12 months before use, ensuring clean-burning, flavorful smoke.

Tip 3: Brine or Cure Your Foods Properly

Proper brining or curing dramatically enhances flavor, tenderness, and safety:

- Brine meats and fish in saltwater mixtures before smoking for added moisture and flavor.
- Cure meats thoroughly (especially important for cold smoking) to ensure safety and enhanced preservation.

Amish wisdom:
For richer flavor, Amish brines traditionally include brown sugar, maple syrup, molasses, herbs (thyme, rosemary), garlic, or peppercorns.

Tip 4: Allow Foods to Dry Before Smoking (Pellicle Formation)

Proper drying creates a pellicle—a slightly sticky surface layer—that ensures smoke adheres better, resulting in enhanced flavor and attractive coloring.

- Allow meats, fish, and poultry to air-dry uncovered in cool, ventilated areas for 1–3 hours before placing them in the smoker.

Amish practical advice:
The pellicle is essential, especially for fish and poultry—never skip this step to ensure optimal results.

Tip 5: Use Gentle, Consistent Smoke

Amish smoking tradition values subtle, consistent smoke rather than thick, billowing clouds:

- Aim for thin, gentle smoke during the entire smoking period, maintaining optimal airflow.
- Thick smoke or excessive smoke leads to bitter flavors and unpleasant aftertastes.

Amish tip:
If smoke becomes thick or harsh, open smoker vents slightly or reduce the amount of wood burning to maintain a gentle, steady smoke stream.

Tip 6: Rotate Foods Regularly

Rotating food ensures even cooking, color, and smoke penetration:

- Rotate or turn meats and cheeses gently every hour, especially in larger smokehouses.
- Use hooks or racks strategically to optimize exposure to smoke and heat.

Amish practical wisdom:
Consistent rotation prevents uneven cooking and helps achieve professional-quality smoked foods.

Tip 7: Patience and Low-and-Slow Approach

Amish smoking emphasizes patience. Properly smoked food takes time to develop rich, deep flavor and perfect texture:

- Never rush the process. Maintain lower, consistent temperatures for prolonged periods.
- Allow enough time to smoke slowly—often several hours longer than planned yields superior results.

Amish traditional advice:
Slow smoking transforms tougher cuts into tender delicacies, rewarding patience with unmatched flavor and texture.

Tip 8: Resting and Cooling Foods After Smoking

Allowing smoked foods proper rest and cooling improves flavor distribution, texture, and moisture retention:

- After removing from the smoker, let meats rest for 10–20 minutes before slicing.
- Cool cheeses and fish completely to room temperature before refrigerating, enhancing texture and flavor.

Amish tip:
Resting periods allow juices to redistribute evenly, ensuring every bite is tender, moist, and flavorful.

Tip 9: Keep Detailed Smoking Records

Documenting your smoking process allows consistent results and easy adjustments for future smoking sessions:

- Record wood type, smoking temperatures, duration, seasoning, brine recipes, and flavor outcomes.
- Note what worked well or what you'd like to change, helping perfect your personal technique over time.

Amish practical advice:
A simple smoking journal becomes a treasured resource, simplifying repeated successes and valuable adjustments.

Tip 10: Safety and Cleanliness Above All

Amish households emphasize food safety and cleanliness as non-negotiable essentials for successful smoking:

- Regularly clean your smokehouse, racks, hooks, and utensils thoroughly.
- Always follow recommended internal cooking temperatures, monitoring carefully for safety.

Amish safety advice:
Never reuse curing brines or marinades—prepare fresh batches each smoking session to ensure safety and consistency.

Amish Quick Reference for Perfect Smoking:

- ✓ Accurate temperature control and monitoring
- ✓ Properly seasoned, dry hardwood selection
- ✓ Thorough brining or curing prior to smoking
- ✓ Allow pellicle formation before smoking
- ✓ Maintain gentle, consistent smoke
- ✓ Regularly rotate or turn food for even smoking
- ✓ Patiently smoke low-and-slow

- ✓ Allow sufficient resting and cooling after smoking
- ✓ Keep detailed records of your smoking process
- ✓ Prioritize safety, cleanliness, and careful handling

By applying these traditional Amish practical tips consistently, you'll master the rewarding art of smoking foods at home. Each batch will reflect deeper experience and improved technique, allowing you to savor delicious, flavorful foods crafted the authentic Amish way—rich in tradition, perfected by practice, and enjoyed across generations.

CHAPTER 4: AMISH PICKLING AND FERMENTING

How to Make Perfect Pickling Brines

Pickling is a timeless tradition among Amish families, turning simple garden produce into delicious, tangy treats preserved safely for year-round enjoyment. Central to every successful pickle recipe is the **brine**—a carefully balanced solution of vinegar, salt, water, sugar, and spices. Growing up Amish, I spent countless hours in my family's kitchen learning the secrets behind making the perfect brine, mastering the exact balance of flavors that ensure crisp, flavorful, and delicious pickles. In this practical guide, I'll share traditional Amish insights and clear, step-by-step methods to help you create consistently perfect pickling brines.

Understanding Amish Pickling Brines

A traditional Amish pickling brine combines three essential elements: **vinegar**, **salt**, and **water**, often complemented by sugar and spices. Each ingredient serves a specific purpose in flavor, preservation, and texture:

- **Vinegar:** Provides necessary acidity, preserves freshness, and adds tangy flavor.
- **Salt:** Enhances flavor, preserves texture, and prevents spoilage by inhibiting harmful bacterial growth.
- **Water:** Balances acidity, ensuring a pleasant taste and preventing overly harsh pickles.
- **Sugar (optional but traditional):** Balances acidity, adds subtle sweetness, and helps retain color and crispness.
- **Spices:** Enhance flavor complexity, including dill, mustard seeds, garlic, peppercorns, cloves, and bay leaves.

Amish practical tip:
Always choose clear, distilled white vinegar (5% acidity) or apple cider vinegar (for milder, sweeter pickles). Avoid vinegars below 5% acidity, as they won't adequately preserve pickles.

Classic Amish All-Purpose Pickling Brine (Ideal for Vegetables)

This versatile brine is perfect for cucumbers, green beans, cauliflower, carrots, onions, peppers, and beets.

Ingredients (makes about 2 quarts of brine):

- 3 cups distilled white vinegar (5% acidity)
- 3 cups water (filtered or distilled preferred)
- ½ cup pickling or kosher salt (non-iodized)
- ¼–½ cup white sugar (adjust to taste; Amish typically use ½ cup)
- 1 tablespoon mustard seeds
- 1 tablespoon whole peppercorns
- 2–3 bay leaves (optional)

- 2 cloves garlic, peeled (optional but traditional)

Step-by-step Preparation:

1. Combine vinegar, water, salt, and sugar in a large non-reactive pot (stainless steel or enamel-coated) over medium heat.
2. Stir gently until salt and sugar fully dissolve, heating until the mixture reaches a gentle simmer (do not boil vigorously).
3. Add mustard seeds, peppercorns, garlic, and bay leaves, simmering gently for 5 minutes to infuse flavors.
4. Remove from heat, allowing brine to cool slightly before pouring over vegetables (hot pack method), or cool fully for refrigerator pickles.

Amish wisdom:
Adjust sugar based on personal taste and pickle type—more sugar balances strong vinegar flavor, while less sugar yields tangier pickles.

Amish Sweet Bread-and-Butter Pickling Brine

Perfect for cucumbers, onions, and peppers, creating classic Amish bread-and-butter pickles.

Ingredients (makes about 2 quarts of brine):

- 3 cups apple cider vinegar (5% acidity)
- 3 cups granulated white sugar
- 2 cups water
- ¼ cup pickling or kosher salt
- 2 tablespoons mustard seeds
- 1 teaspoon celery seeds
- 1 teaspoon ground turmeric (optional for color)

Step-by-step Preparation:

1. Combine vinegar, sugar, water, salt, mustard seeds, celery seeds, and turmeric in a large non-reactive pot.

2. Heat gently, stirring frequently, until sugar and salt fully dissolve and brine reaches a simmer.
3. Allow to simmer gently 3–5 minutes, ensuring flavors fully blend.
4. Remove from heat and pour immediately over prepared vegetables in sterilized jars (hot pack method).

Amish practical tip:
Use turmeric sparingly; it provides attractive color but can become overpowering if used excessively.

Amish Dill Pickle Brine (Perfect for Cucumbers and Beans)

Ideal for crunchy dill pickles, green beans, cauliflower, or carrots.

Ingredients (makes about 2 quarts of brine):

- 3 cups distilled white vinegar (5% acidity)
- 3 cups water
- ⅓ cup pickling or kosher salt
- 2 tablespoons granulated sugar (optional)
- 2 tablespoons dill seeds or fresh dill sprigs
- 1 tablespoon mustard seeds
- 4 cloves garlic, peeled and sliced (optional but traditional)

Step-by-step Preparation:

1. Combine vinegar, water, salt, sugar, dill seeds, mustard seeds, and garlic in a non-reactive pot.
2. Bring mixture gently to a simmer, stirring occasionally to dissolve salt and sugar.
3. Simmer brine gently for 5 minutes to fully infuse dill and garlic flavors.
4. Remove from heat, immediately pour over vegetables packed tightly in sterilized jars (hot pack method).

Amish wisdom:
Fresh dill sprigs placed directly into jars before adding vegetables and brine provide authentic Amish dill pickle flavor and appearance.

Amish Tips for Creating Perfect Brines:

- Always use clean, non-reactive cookware (stainless steel or enamel) to prevent metallic or off-flavors.

- Adjust spices and sweetness based on family preferences, keeping careful notes to consistently reproduce favorite recipes.

- Allow brines to cool slightly before pouring into jars to minimize jar cracking risk, though jars should still be hot and sterilized for best sealing.

Brine Troubleshooting (Amish Quick Reference):

- **Too sour:** Increase water or sugar slightly next batch to balance acidity.

- **Too salty:** Slightly reduce salt and increase water proportionally.

- **Cloudy brine:** Use filtered water or avoid iodized table salt; cloudiness doesn't affect safety but influences appearance.

- **Soft pickles:** Use less sugar or add grape leaves, bay leaves, or alum (traditional Amish methods) to improve crispness.

Amish Quick Checklist for Perfect Pickling Brines:

- ✓ Use vinegar (5% acidity) for safe preservation.

- ✓ Balance salt, sugar, and water carefully.

- ✓ Infuse spices gently for optimal flavor.

- ✓ Use clean, sterilized jars and lids for safety and longevity.

- ✓ Adjust ingredients thoughtfully for preferred flavor profiles.

By following these practical, traditional Amish guidelines, you'll create consistently perfect pickling brines that transform simple vegetables into flavorful treats. Every jar of pickles becomes an opportunity to preserve wholesome food, connect with Amish heritage, and share the joy of homemade pickles with your family season after season.

Practical Recipes for Quick Pickles

In Amish kitchens, quick pickles—also called refrigerator pickles—have long been a favorite method for transforming fresh produce into flavorful, crisp, tangy treats in just a few hours or days. Growing up Amish, I watched my mother prepare quick pickles regularly, especially during harvest season. They're easy to prepare, require minimal ingredients, and offer immediate enjoyment without extensive canning processes. In this section, I'll share traditional Amish quick pickle recipes that you can prepare simply and enjoy quickly.

Recipe 1: Amish Quick Refrigerator Dill Pickles

Ingredients (makes 2 quart-sized jars):

- 8–10 small to medium cucumbers, sliced or quartered lengthwise
- 2 cups distilled white vinegar (5% acidity)
- 2 cups water
- 2 tablespoons pickling salt (non-iodized)
- 2 tablespoons sugar (optional but traditional)
- 4 cloves garlic, peeled and slightly crushed
- 1 tablespoon mustard seeds
- 4 sprigs fresh dill or 1 tablespoon dill seeds

Step-by-step Instructions:

1. Wash cucumbers thoroughly and slice or quarter lengthwise.
2. In a saucepan, combine vinegar, water, pickling salt, and sugar. Heat gently until salt and sugar dissolve. Cool briefly.
3. In clean quart jars, add garlic cloves, mustard seeds, and dill sprigs or seeds.
4. Pack cucumbers tightly into jars, leaving ½-inch headspace at the top.
5. Pour the warm brine over cucumbers, covering them fully.
6. Seal jars with lids tightly, allow them to cool slightly, then refrigerate immediately.

7. Let them sit in the refrigerator for at least 24 hours before enjoying; flavor improves after 2–3 days.

Amish practical tip:
Enjoy refrigerator dill pickles within 4–6 weeks for best flavor and crispness.

Recipe 2: Amish Quick Bread-and-Butter Pickles

Ingredients (makes 2 quart-sized jars):

- 8 medium-sized cucumbers, thinly sliced
- 1 medium onion, thinly sliced
- 1½ cups apple cider vinegar (5% acidity)
- 1½ cups granulated sugar
- 1 cup water
- 1 tablespoon pickling or kosher salt
- 2 teaspoons mustard seeds
- 1 teaspoon celery seeds
- ¼ teaspoon turmeric powder (optional for color)

Step-by-step Instructions:

1. Combine cucumber and onion slices in a large bowl.
2. In a saucepan, combine vinegar, sugar, water, salt, mustard seeds, celery seeds, and turmeric. Heat gently, stirring, until sugar dissolves.
3. Pour warm brine over cucumber-onion mixture. Stir gently and allow to sit 30 minutes at room temperature.
4. Pack cucumbers and onions tightly into clean jars, pouring the brine over the top.
5. Seal jars tightly and refrigerate at least 24 hours before serving.

Amish practical tip:
Quick bread-and-butter pickles are best consumed within 4–6 weeks, refrigerated.

Recipe 3: Amish Quick Pickled Green Beans ("Dilly Beans")

Ingredients (makes 2 pint-sized jars):

- 1 pound fresh green beans, trimmed to fit jars
- 1½ cups distilled white vinegar (5% acidity)
- 1½ cups water
- 1½ tablespoons pickling or kosher salt
- 2 cloves garlic, peeled
- 2 teaspoons mustard seeds
- 2 sprigs fresh dill or 1 teaspoon dill seeds
- ½ teaspoon red pepper flakes (optional for spice)

Step-by-step Instructions:

1. Wash and trim green beans to fit pint jars.
2. Combine vinegar, water, and salt in a saucepan, heating gently until salt dissolves. Cool slightly.
3. Place garlic, mustard seeds, dill, and red pepper flakes (optional) into clean pint jars.
4. Pack green beans upright, tightly into jars, leaving ½-inch headspace.
5. Pour warm brine into jars, completely covering green beans.
6. Seal jars tightly, refrigerate immediately, and let sit for 24–48 hours before enjoying.

Amish tip:
These dilly beans remain crisp and flavorful for 4–6 weeks refrigerated.

Recipe 4: Amish Quick Pickled Red Onions

Ingredients (makes 1 quart-sized jar):

- 2 large red onions, thinly sliced
- 1 cup apple cider vinegar (5% acidity)

- 1 cup water
- 2 tablespoons granulated sugar
- 1½ teaspoons pickling or kosher salt
- 1 teaspoon whole peppercorns
- 1–2 bay leaves (optional)

Step-by-step Instructions:

1. Thinly slice red onions and pack tightly into a clean quart jar.
2. Combine vinegar, water, sugar, salt, peppercorns, and bay leaves in a saucepan. Heat gently until salt and sugar dissolve.
3. Pour warm brine over onions, covering fully. Seal tightly.
4. Refrigerate immediately, allowing at least 24 hours before enjoying. Flavor and color intensify after 2–3 days.

Amish practical advice:
Quick pickled onions add flavor to sandwiches, salads, and cheese boards and keep refrigerated up to 4 weeks.

Amish Quick-Pickling Tips for Best Results:

- Always use fresh, firm vegetables for crisp pickles.
- Allow pickles to rest in brine at least 24–48 hours before eating, improving flavor significantly.
- Keep pickles refrigerated at all times—quick pickles aren't shelf-stable like canned pickles.
- Experiment with different spices and herbs to find your family's favorite combination (garlic, mustard seeds, dill, peppercorns, or cloves).

Common Quick Pickle Problems & Amish Solutions:

- **Soft pickles:**
  Use fresh produce, chill quickly, and add grape leaves or bay leaves to jars to maintain crispness.

- **Too salty:**
  Reduce salt slightly in next batches or rinse produce briefly before brining.

- **Cloudy brine:**
  Use filtered water and avoid iodized table salt; slight cloudiness is normal, safe, and common.

Amish Quick Reference—Pickle Storage and Shelf-Life:

- Store all quick pickles refrigerated immediately after preparation.
- Consume quick pickles ideally within 4–6 weeks.
- Clearly label jars with contents and date prepared for easy reference.

By following these traditional Amish quick pickle recipes and practical advice, you'll easily transform fresh garden produce into delicious treats. Each jar is an opportunity to preserve flavors, create satisfying meals, and share the joy of homemade pickles with your family and friends—quickly, easily, and authentically Amish.

Easy Fermented Vegetables Step-by-Step

Fermentation has long been a cherished practice in Amish households, transforming simple garden vegetables into nutritious, flavorful, and health-promoting foods. Growing up Amish, I watched my grandmother carefully ferment vegetables each season—patiently preparing jars of tangy sauerkraut, crunchy carrots, and flavorful fermented cucumbers. These practical step-by-step instructions will guide you in successfully fermenting vegetables, enabling you to preserve food naturally while enriching your diet with beneficial probiotics and delightful taste.

Why Amish Families Love Fermented Vegetables

Fermented vegetables provide both preservation and health benefits:

- **Enhanced nutrition:** Fermentation increases vitamins and beneficial probiotics.
- **Improved digestion:** Probiotics aid digestive health and support immunity.
- **Extended shelf-life:** Fermentation naturally preserves vegetables safely without refrigeration (short-term).

Step-by-Step Amish Guide to Fermented Vegetables

Step 1: Choosing Fresh Vegetables

Select fresh, firm, and healthy vegetables directly from your garden, farmers market, or trusted source:

Best vegetables for fermenting:

- Cabbage (classic Amish sauerkraut)
- Cucumbers (fermented pickles)
- Carrots
- Green beans
- Cauliflower
- Radishes

- Beets
- Onions

Amish practical tip:
Use freshly harvested vegetables; they ferment faster and maintain crisp texture and vibrant flavor.

Step 2: Preparing Vegetables for Fermentation

- Wash vegetables thoroughly in cool water to remove dirt and impurities.
- Trim and discard any damaged or bruised sections.
- Slice or chop vegetables evenly to ensure consistent fermentation.

Traditional Amish preparation examples:

- **Cabbage:** Shred finely or slice thinly for sauerkraut.
- **Cucumbers:** Leave whole (small ones) or slice lengthwise into spears.
- **Carrots, radishes, cauliflower:** Cut into uniform-sized pieces or rounds.

Step 3: Making the Brine (Salt-Water Solution)

Proper brine concentration is crucial for successful fermentation and food safety:

Basic Amish Brine Recipe (2%–3% solution):

- 1 quart filtered or distilled water (avoid chlorinated tap water)
- 1½–2 tablespoons kosher or pickling salt (non-iodized)

Step-by-step Instructions:

1. Heat water slightly to dissolve salt fully, then cool to room temperature.
2. Ensure brine is completely cooled before pouring onto vegetables.

Amish practical wisdom:
Never use iodized salt—iodine inhibits fermentation and can affect flavor.

Step 4: Packing Vegetables for Fermentation

- Pack prepared vegetables tightly into clean glass jars or ceramic fermentation crocks, leaving approximately 1–2 inches of headspace at the top.
- Pour cooled brine over vegetables until fully submerged.
- Vegetables must remain below brine surface to prevent mold and spoilage.

Amish tip:
Use fermentation weights, a clean ceramic plate, or cabbage leaves to hold vegetables beneath the brine.

Step 5: Beginning the Fermentation Process

- Cover jars loosely with clean cloth, coffee filters, or specially designed fermentation lids to allow airflow while keeping contaminants out.

- Secure covers with rubber bands or rings.

Ideal Amish fermentation conditions:

- Keep jars at stable room temperature (60–75°F / 16–24°C) away from direct sunlight.

- Avoid excessive heat or temperature fluctuations, which negatively affect fermentation quality.

Step 6: Monitoring Fermentation (Traditional Amish Method)

- During fermentation, bubbles forming indicate active fermentation—this is normal and desirable.

- Vegetables typically ferment in 3–14 days depending on type and desired flavor intensity:
    - Sauerkraut: 1–3 weeks
    - Cucumbers, carrots, beans: 5–10 days
    - Radishes, cauliflower: 5–7 days

- Taste vegetables every few days, using clean utensils, to gauge readiness.

Amish practical tip:
Fermentation slows significantly in colder conditions and accelerates in warmer temperatures—monitor closely for desired flavor.

Step 7: Completing Fermentation and Refrigeration

- When vegetables reach your preferred flavor (tangy and slightly sour), replace cloth covers with tight-fitting lids and refrigerate immediately.

- Refrigeration slows further fermentation, preserving flavor and texture at optimal levels.

Amish wisdom:
Fermented vegetables kept refrigerated stay fresh and flavorful for several months.

Easy Amish Recipe Examples for Fermented Vegetables:

Amish Fermented Carrots and Dill

Ingredients:

- 1 pound fresh carrots, sliced into sticks or rounds
- 2 cloves garlic, peeled
- 1 tablespoon dill seeds or 2–3 sprigs fresh dill
- Basic brine (2 tablespoons salt per quart water)

Preparation:

1. Pack carrots tightly into jars, adding garlic and dill evenly.
2. Pour cooled brine over carrots, submerging fully.
3. Cover with cloth, ferment at room temperature for 5–7 days, then refrigerate.

Amish Simple Fermented Green Beans

Ingredients:

- 1 pound fresh green beans, trimmed
- 2 cloves garlic, peeled
- 1 teaspoon red pepper flakes (optional for spice)
- Basic brine (2 tablespoons salt per quart water)

Preparation:

1. Pack beans upright tightly in jars, adding garlic and pepper flakes evenly.
2. Submerge fully in cooled brine.
3. Ferment 7–10 days, then refrigerate.

Amish Troubleshooting Tips for Fermented Vegetables:

- **White film or mold:**
  A harmless white film (kahm yeast) can occur; skim away gently. Discard vegetables immediately if mold is dark, black, or fuzzy.

- **Too salty:**
  Reduce salt slightly in the next batch; rinse vegetables briefly before serving.

- **Vegetables floating:**
  Use fermentation weights or cabbage leaves to submerge vegetables properly.

Amish Quick Reference for Successful Fermentation:

- ✓ Use fresh vegetables and non-iodized salt.
- ✓ Maintain proper brine concentration (2%–3%).
- ✓ Keep vegetables fully submerged under brine.
- ✓ Ferment at stable room temperatures.
- ✓ Refrigerate after achieving desired flavor.

By following these practical, step-by-step Amish fermentation guidelines, you'll easily create nutritious, flavorful fermented vegetables at home. This traditional method not only preserves seasonal abundance but also promotes health, connects you with Amish culinary heritage, and provides the deep satisfaction of crafting wholesome, delicious foods through simple, natural fermentation techniques.

Sauerkraut the Amish Way

Sauerkraut is one of the most beloved and traditional fermented foods in Amish culture, prized for its flavor, simplicity, and numerous health benefits. Growing up Amish, making sauerkraut was more than a food preservation technique—it was a treasured seasonal tradition that brought our family together, turning simple cabbage into tangy, nourishing, probiotic-rich goodness. In this practical guide, I'll share the authentic Amish method for making perfect sauerkraut step-by-step, ensuring delicious results every time.

Why Amish Families Love Sauerkraut

Sauerkraut has long been valued in Amish communities because it:

- Provides essential probiotics and vitamins.
- Supports healthy digestion and immunity.
- Offers easy and economical long-term preservation of cabbage harvest.
- Adds flavorful depth to meals year-round.

Amish Sauerkraut Step-by-Step Guide

Step 1: Choosing and Preparing Cabbage

- Select fresh, firm heads of cabbage, ideally harvested recently from your garden or local farm.
- Rinse cabbage heads well under cool water.
- Remove and discard outer leaves that are damaged or wilted.

Amish practical tip:
Save a few large, clean outer cabbage leaves to cover shredded cabbage later, helping maintain submerged fermentation.

Step 2: Shredding the Cabbage

- Cut cabbage heads into quarters, removing and discarding the tough inner core.
- Finely shred cabbage using a sharp knife, mandoline, or traditional Amish cabbage shredder.
- Uniform, fine shreds help ferment cabbage evenly and quickly.

Amish wisdom:
Aim for shreds approximately 1/8-inch (3mm) thick—thin enough to ferment well yet maintain some texture after fermentation.

Step 3: Adding Salt to the Shredded Cabbage

- Place shredded cabbage in a large bowl, layering cabbage with salt evenly as you go.
- Use approximately 1½–2 tablespoons kosher or pickling salt (non-iodized) per 3 pounds of cabbage.

Traditional Amish Salt Ratio:

- For every 5 pounds cabbage: use about 3 tablespoons salt (roughly 2% brine ratio).

Step 4: Massaging and Packing the Cabbage

- Massage cabbage vigorously with your hands, squeezing and kneading until it releases natural juices (takes about 5–10 minutes).
- The cabbage is ready when there is enough juice to cover the cabbage when packed tightly.
- Pack cabbage tightly into clean jars or a traditional ceramic crock, pressing firmly to remove air pockets and keep cabbage submerged beneath the juices.

Amish tip:
A wooden spoon or sauerkraut tamper helps press cabbage firmly and evenly into the crock or jar.

Step 5: Covering the Sauerkraut for Fermentation

- Place reserved cabbage leaves or a clean ceramic plate directly over the shredded cabbage to hold it beneath the liquid.
- Weigh down cabbage with fermentation weights, clean stones, or a sealed jar filled with water.
- Ensure all cabbage remains submerged in its own brine throughout fermentation—this prevents spoilage.

Step 6: Fermenting Your Sauerkraut

- Cover jars or crock loosely with a clean cloth or specialized fermentation lid to allow airflow and release fermentation gases.
- Ferment sauerkraut at consistent room temperature (60–75°F / 16–24°C), away from direct sunlight.
- Allow sauerkraut to ferment at least 7–14 days. Taste regularly—Amish tradition typically ferments sauerkraut 2–4 weeks for optimal flavor and probiotic benefits.

Amish wisdom:
Warmer conditions ferment faster; cooler conditions slow fermentation—adjust fermentation time accordingly.

Step 7: Monitoring and Checking Sauerkraut

- Check sauerkraut every 2–3 days during fermentation.
- Small bubbles indicate healthy fermentation.
- Remove any harmless white yeast (kahm yeast) carefully with a clean spoon; this is normal and safe.
- Discard sauerkraut if dark, fuzzy, or moldy patches appear.

Amish practical tip:
Always use clean utensils to sample sauerkraut to avoid contamination.

Step 8: Finishing Fermentation and Refrigeration

- Once sauerkraut reaches your preferred tangy flavor and crunchy texture, remove fermentation weights, cover jars tightly, and refrigerate immediately.
- Refrigeration slows fermentation, maintaining flavor and crispness.

Amish practical advice:
Properly fermented sauerkraut stored in the refrigerator remains fresh and tasty for 4–6 months or longer.

Traditional Amish Sauerkraut Variations (Optional but Delicious):

Enhance flavor and nutrition by adding these traditional Amish additions:

- **Caraway seeds:** 1–2 teaspoons per cabbage head for traditional flavor.
- **Apples:** Finely sliced apples mixed with cabbage add sweetness.
- **Onions or garlic:** Add finely sliced onions or garlic cloves for savory depth.

Amish Sauerkraut Troubleshooting Guide:

- **Not enough juice to cover cabbage:**
  Massage cabbage longer or add a little saltwater brine (2 teaspoons salt per cup water) to cover cabbage fully.

- **Soft or mushy texture:**
  Reduce fermentation time or ferment in slightly cooler temperatures.
- **Too salty:**
  Rinse sauerkraut briefly in cold water before serving, or slightly reduce salt next time.

How Amish Families Serve and Enjoy Sauerkraut:

Sauerkraut traditionally accompanies:

- Pork roast or sausages.
- Mashed potatoes (a classic Amish comfort meal).
- Added to soups and stews for tangy richness.
- Served alongside hearty sandwiches or as a simple side dish.

Amish Quick Checklist for Perfect Sauerkraut:

- ✓ Fresh cabbage shredded finely and evenly
- ✓ Proper salt ratio (about 2% salt by weight)
- ✓ Thorough massaging to release cabbage juices
- ✓ Cabbage fully submerged in brine during fermentation
- ✓ Stable room temperature during fermentation
- ✓ Regular checks for taste and texture
- ✓ Immediate refrigeration once desired flavor is reached

By following these practical, traditional Amish instructions, you'll create delicious, nutritious sauerkraut easily and confidently. Each batch connects you to the heritage of Amish cooking, nourishing your family with wholesome probiotics, authentic flavor, and the satisfaction that comes from crafting traditional, homemade fermented foods—exactly as Amish families have done for generations.

Common Issues in Pickling and How to Solve Them

Amish households have long treasured the art of pickling, transforming simple garden produce into flavorful preserves. However, even experienced Amish homemakers occasionally encounter challenges in pickling. Growing up Amish, I learned practical ways to identify, understand, and quickly correct common pickling problems. In this practical guide, I'll share traditional Amish insights and clear solutions to help you consistently create delicious, safe, and high-quality pickles.

Issue 1: Soft or Mushy Pickles

Possible Causes:

- Overripe vegetables
- Insufficient salt or vinegar in brine
- Excessive heat or prolonged processing time during canning
- Using table salt with iodine or additives

Amish Solutions:

- Always select fresh, firm, and slightly underripe produce.
- Use only pickling salt (non-iodized), kosher salt, or pure sea salt.
- Limit heating time—process jars only as long as necessary.
- Add grape leaves, bay leaves, or natural crisping agents (like food-grade calcium chloride) to maintain crispness.

Amish Practical Tip:
Including grape leaves in each jar is a traditional Amish secret to consistently crisp pickles.

Issue 2: Cloudy Pickle Brine

Possible Causes:

- Using hard or chlorinated water
- Table salt containing iodine or anti-caking additives

- Yeast growth (kahm yeast) during fermentation (harmless but cloudy)

Amish Solutions:

- Use filtered, distilled, or bottled water in your brines.
- Choose only pickling salt, kosher salt, or pure sea salt without additives.
- Cloudiness from kahm yeast is normal—skim gently from surface; pickles remain safe and delicious.

Amish Practical Advice:
Cloudy brine from minerals or yeast is harmless but affects appearance. Always label jars clearly to note safe, though cloudy, batches.

Issue 3: Pickles Too Salty or Vinegary

Possible Causes:

- Brine concentration too strong (too much salt or vinegar)
- Inadequate rinsing or brine measurement mistakes

Amish Solutions:

- Double-check brine measurements carefully each batch.
- Briefly rinse salty pickles under cool water before serving, reducing saltiness.
- Slightly reduce salt or vinegar in future brine recipes (but never below safe preservation standards—vinegar must be at least 5% acidity).

Amish Wisdom:
Balancing salt, vinegar, and sugar carefully creates delicious pickles; always measure ingredients precisely.

Issue 4: Pickles Floating in the Jar

Possible Causes:

- Vegetables loosely packed
- Vegetables not weighted or adequately submerged in brine

Amish Solutions:

- Pack vegetables tightly into jars, minimizing air pockets.
- Use weights or cabbage leaves to ensure vegetables remain submerged.
- Trim vegetables into uniform sizes for better packing.

Amish Practical Tip:
Tightly packed jars help vegetables absorb brine better, resulting in improved flavor and reduced floating.

Issue 5: Darkened or Discolored Pickles

Possible Causes:

- Vegetables exposed to air or not fully submerged
- Using metal utensils or reactive cookware
- Exposure to direct sunlight during storage

Amish Solutions:

- Fully submerge vegetables beneath brine during pickling and storage.
- Use stainless steel, enamel-coated, glass, or ceramic utensils and pots only.
- Store pickles in dark, cool locations away from sunlight.

Amish Practical Advice:
Darkened pickles can still be safe to eat, but always use your senses to confirm freshness and discard if in doubt.

Issue 6: Off-Flavors or Unpleasant Smells

Possible Causes:

- Contamination from unclean jars or utensils
- Inadequate acidity (vinegar less than 5% acidity)
- Spoilage from improper sealing or storage

Amish Solutions:

- Always sterilize jars, utensils, and equipment thoroughly before pickling.
- Use vinegar consistently at 5% acidity or higher for safe preservation.
- Immediately discard pickles with foul odors, slimy textures, or suspicious mold growth.

Amish Practical Tip:
Trust your senses—Amish wisdom states that unpleasant odors or sliminess clearly indicate spoilage and should never be consumed.

Issue 7: Mold Growth on Surface

Possible Causes:

- Vegetables not fully submerged
- Containers or utensils improperly cleaned
- Insufficient salt or vinegar content

Amish Solutions:

- Always ensure vegetables remain fully submerged beneath brine.
- Skim harmless white mold (kahm yeast) carefully and discard if dark mold forms.
- Thoroughly sanitize jars, lids, and utensils to prevent contamination.

Amish Safety Advice:
Always discard pickles immediately if you see black, fuzzy, or suspicious mold—this indicates spoilage and potential danger.

Issue 8: Jars Not Sealing Properly

Possible Causes:

- Dirty or chipped jar rims
- Using old or improperly prepared lids
- Incorrect headspace in jars

Amish Solutions:

- Wipe jar rims meticulously before sealing, discarding chipped jars.
- Always use fresh, properly prepared lids and bands.
- Maintain recommended headspace (usually ½ inch) in jars.

Amish Practical Advice:
Immediately refrigerate jars that don't seal properly and consume within two weeks, or reprocess promptly using new lids.

Amish Quick Reference—Avoiding Pickling Problems:

- ✓ Select fresh, firm vegetables.
- ✓ Use precise brine measurements.
- ✓ Maintain proper vinegar (minimum 5% acidity) and salt levels.
- ✓ Pack vegetables tightly, ensuring they stay submerged.
- ✓ Sterilize jars and utensils carefully.
- ✓ Store pickles in cool, dark conditions.
- ✓ Regularly check jars for signs of spoilage or mold.

By understanding these common pickling challenges and applying traditional Amish solutions, you'll confidently create delicious, crisp, and safely preserved pickles season after season. With each successful jar, you'll preserve the bounty of the harvest, nourish your family, and carry forward a cherished Amish culinary tradition.

Best Practices for Storing Pickled and Fermented Foods

In Amish homes, the art of pickling and fermenting goes beyond preserving fresh produce; it also includes the critical step of proper storage. Growing up Amish, I learned that careful, mindful storage practices ensure pickled and fermented foods maintain their flavor, nutritional value, texture, and safety throughout the year. Here, I'll share traditional Amish insights and practical methods for properly storing pickled and fermented foods, helping you preserve your carefully prepared jars at their very best.

Ideal Storage Conditions

For optimal preservation, pickled and fermented foods require a cool, dark, and dry environment. Amish families traditionally use root cellars, basements, or dedicated pantry spaces, offering ideal conditions for long-term storage.

- **Temperature:**
  Ideal storage temperatures range from 40°F–60°F (4°C–16°C). Refrigeration is best for fermented vegetables, while canned pickles store well in slightly warmer pantry conditions.

- **Darkness:**
  Store jars away from direct sunlight or bright artificial lights, which degrade quality, flavor, and color over time.

- **Humidity:**
  Maintain moderate humidity (50%–65%) to prevent rust on jar lids and deterioration of labels.

Amish practical tip:
If lacking a cellar or basement, designate a pantry cupboard or closet away from ovens, dishwashers, or windows, providing stable temperature and darkness.

Storing Pickled Foods (Canned Method)

Pickled vegetables processed using water-bath canning methods can be safely stored at room temperature, provided the following practices are maintained:

- **Ensure Proper Sealing:**
  Check seals by pressing the jar lids gently. Properly sealed lids are firm and concave without any "pop" or movement.

- **Remove Metal Bands for Storage:**
  After jars cool and seal (24 hours), remove metal bands before storing. This helps prevent rust and allows easy detection of unsealed jars.
- **Label Clearly:**
  Label each jar clearly with the date and contents to ensure proper rotation—always consuming older jars first.
- **Inspect Regularly:**
  Periodically inspect jars for signs of spoilage, such as bulging lids, leaks, or discoloration. Immediately discard questionable jars.

Amish practical advice:
Home-canned pickles retain optimal quality for up to 1–2 years when properly stored.

Storing Fermented Vegetables (Refrigeration Required)

Fermented vegetables differ from pickled (vinegar-canned) vegetables because fermentation relies on active cultures and does not include a heat-sealing step. They require refrigeration for safe storage and flavor preservation.

- **Immediate Refrigeration:**
  Refrigerate fermented vegetables immediately after fermentation is complete. This slows down fermentation, stabilizes flavor, and maintains crisp texture.
- **Use Tight-Fitting Lids:**
  After fermentation finishes, secure jars with tight-fitting lids to prevent further oxygen exposure and minimize mold risks.
- **Monitor Regularly:**
  Check jars monthly, removing any harmless white yeast (kahm yeast). Discard immediately if dark mold or unpleasant odors occur.

Amish practical advice:
Fermented vegetables stored refrigerated remain safe and flavorful for 4–6 months or longer.

Storing Quick (Refrigerator) Pickles

Quick refrigerator pickles are not shelf-stable like traditional canned pickles and must be stored in refrigeration at all times:

- **Keep Refrigerated Constantly:**
  Store quick pickles tightly sealed in the refrigerator immediately after preparation.

- **Consume Within 4–6 Weeks:**
  Quick pickles maintain optimal flavor, crispness, and safety for approximately 4–6 weeks refrigerated.

- **Clearly Label:**
  Label jars clearly with preparation dates for easy tracking and timely consumption.

Amish Tips for Long-Term Storage Success

- **Proper Rotation ("First-In, First-Out"):**
  Always consume older jars first, clearly labeling jars with dates. This practice maintains optimal freshness and reduces waste.

- **Regular Inspection and Cleaning:**
  Periodically clean storage areas, removing dust and inspecting jars for signs of spoilage or damage.

- **Maintain Cleanliness:**
  Keep shelves and jars clean and dry to prevent mold growth or pests attracted by residue or moisture.

Recognizing Spoilage—Traditional Amish Wisdom

Always trust your senses. Traditional Amish households rely on simple sensory tests to detect spoilage:

- **Visual Inspection:**
  Discard jars immediately if lids bulge, brine leaks, or visible mold forms inside the jars.

- **Smell:**
  Never consume pickled or fermented foods with off-putting odors, rotten smells, or unusual fermentation aromas.

- **Texture and Appearance:**
  Softness, sliminess, or abnormal discoloration indicates spoilage. Discard without tasting.

Amish Practical Tip:
If ever unsure, discard questionable food—Amish families value safety above saving a single jar.

Amish Quick Checklist for Proper Storage of Pickled and Fermented Foods:

- √ Cool, dark, dry storage environment (40°F–60°F).
- √ Clearly labeled jars (contents and date).
- √ Immediate refrigeration of fermented vegetables and quick pickles.
- √ Regular inspection for spoilage signs.
- √ Proper rotation system ("first-in, first-out").

By following these traditional Amish storage guidelines, you ensure your carefully pickled and fermented foods remain safe, flavorful, and enjoyable throughout the year. Each jar preserved becomes more than food—it's a reflection of care, practicality, and heritage, allowing you to savor delicious, homemade Amish goodness in every season.

CHAPTER 5: AMISH METHODS FOR DRYING FOODS

Simple Outdoor and Indoor Drying Setups

Drying food has been an essential part of Amish tradition for generations, providing a straightforward and reliable method for preserving the bounty of summer gardens and orchards. Growing up Amish, I remember how my mother would carefully prepare and dry fresh fruits, vegetables, and herbs, ensuring nutritious and flavorful ingredients were always available, even through long winters. In this practical guide, I'll show you exactly how to create simple yet effective outdoor and indoor drying setups inspired by authentic Amish methods, making drying foods easy, efficient, and safe.

Outdoor Drying Methods: Amish Practical Setups

Setup 1: Amish-Style Drying Racks or Screens

In Amish communities, drying racks or screens placed outdoors under the sun have long been used to naturally dry produce.

Materials Needed:

- Wooden frames (untreated hardwood, like oak, pine, or maple)
- Stainless-steel or food-grade plastic mesh screens
- Small nails, staples, or screws
- Cheesecloth or muslin (optional, to protect from insects)

Step-by-Step Instructions:

1. Construct simple wooden frames (typically about 2 feet by 3 feet or larger).
2. Stretch and attach food-grade screens securely across the frames using staples or nails.
3. Place freshly prepared fruits, vegetables, or herbs in a single, even layer on screens, ensuring good airflow around each piece.
4. Set racks outside on warm, sunny days, ideally placed on raised supports like bricks, stones, or sawhorses for maximum airflow.
5. Cover lightly with cheesecloth or muslin to protect from insects and birds, allowing sun and air to circulate freely.

Amish Practical Tip:
Regularly turn food (every few hours) to ensure even drying on all sides and optimal results.

Setup 2: Hanging Bundles or Strings (Ideal for Herbs, Chilies, and Onions)

Traditionally, Amish families hang herbs, onions, garlic, and peppers in bundles to dry naturally.

Materials Needed:

- Clean twine or cotton string
- Hooks, wooden beams, or drying rods

- Freshly harvested herbs, peppers, onions, garlic bulbs

Step-by-Step Instructions:

1. Tie harvested herbs, peppers, garlic, or onions securely into small bundles using twine.
2. Suspend bundles in shaded areas outdoors, protected from rain and direct harsh sun.
3. Ensure sufficient airflow around bundles to prevent mold growth.
4. Allow drying naturally outdoors for several days or weeks, depending on the moisture content and weather conditions.

Amish Wisdom:
Hang bundles under porch roofs, eaves, or sheltered outdoor areas—this allows air circulation, protects from weather, and results in aromatic, well-preserved herbs and vegetables.

Indoor Drying Methods: Traditional Amish Techniques

Setup 1: Indoor Drying Racks or Screens (Near Windows)

Ideal during cooler seasons or unpredictable weather, indoor drying screens placed near windows provide natural drying.

Materials Needed:

- Same wooden frames and screens as outdoor drying setup
- Shelving or tables near sunny windows
- Small electric fan (optional, to improve airflow)

Step-by-Step Instructions:

1. Arrange food evenly on mesh screens.
2. Position racks near south-facing windows or well-lit areas receiving direct sunlight.
3. Rotate and turn food regularly, ensuring even drying and preventing mold or spoilage.
4. Optionally, run a small fan nearby on low speed to increase airflow and reduce drying times.

Amish Practical Advice:
Indoor drying typically takes longer than outdoor drying—patience and careful monitoring ensure excellent results.

Setup 2: Traditional Amish Oven Drying

Used historically by Amish families when outdoor drying wasn't possible or practical.

Materials Needed:

- Standard home oven (gas or electric)
- Baking trays lined with parchment paper or mesh drying racks

Step-by-Step Instructions:

1. Preheat oven to lowest temperature (usually around 120°F–150°F / 50°C–65°C).
2. Spread prepared fruits, vegetables, or herbs evenly on trays, leaving ample space for air circulation.
3. Place trays into oven, keeping door slightly ajar (use a wooden spoon handle to keep it slightly open), allowing moisture to escape and fresh air to circulate.
4. Regularly rotate trays and gently turn food pieces to dry evenly.
5. Drying typically takes several hours (4–12 hours), depending on produce and oven efficiency.

Amish Practical Tip:
Oven drying requires careful attention—always maintain low heat to prevent food from cooking rather than drying.

Setup 3: Woodstove or Fireplace Drying (Classic Amish Method)

Many Amish households traditionally use the warmth of woodstoves or fireplaces during cooler months to dry herbs and produce.

Materials Needed:

- Sturdy string or twine for hanging

- Herbs, apple slices, peppers, onions, or garlic bulbs
- Drying rack or hooks suspended above the stove or fireplace (at a safe distance)

Step-by-Step Instructions:

1. Prepare produce or herbs, tying into small, even bundles.
2. Hang securely on hooks or racks, ensuring adequate distance from heat sources to avoid scorching or burning.
3. Drying gently occurs from ambient warmth and airflow, usually taking several days.
4. Monitor regularly, rotating bundles to promote even drying.

Amish Wisdom:
Always practice caution when drying above heat sources—maintain safe distances and careful monitoring.

Amish Practical Safety Tips for Food Drying:

- Always select clean, fresh, undamaged produce for drying.
- Maintain adequate airflow around drying food.
- Protect drying foods from insects, dust, and pests using muslin or cheesecloth covers.
- Never leave oven-drying or heat-source drying setups unattended for extended periods.
- Monitor drying closely—remove dried items promptly to avoid overdrying or burning.

Quick Amish Reference—Drying Conditions and Times:

- **Fruits:** Require consistent airflow and warmth, usually 6–48 hours depending on moisture content.
- **Vegetables:** Typically dry in 6–36 hours; cut vegetables evenly for uniform drying.

- **Herbs:** Quickest drying times—typically 1–4 days, depending on leaf thickness and humidity.

Traditional Amish Checklist for Simple Drying Setups:

- ✓ Construct simple drying racks or screens using safe, untreated materials.
- ✓ Choose optimal drying location (outdoor or indoor) based on weather conditions and produce type.
- ✓ Ensure constant airflow and gentle, even warmth.
- ✓ Rotate and inspect regularly for consistent drying.
- ✓ Store dried goods promptly after fully dry.

By following these straightforward Amish methods, you'll easily set up effective outdoor or indoor drying spaces, allowing you to preserve the bounty of your garden or harvest naturally and safely. Each batch of dried food you prepare preserves nutritious and flavorful ingredients, connects you with timeless Amish heritage, and offers the satisfaction of mastering a simple yet highly effective food preservation skill used by generations of Amish families.

Best Techniques for Drying Fruits, Vegetables, and Herbs

Drying fruits, vegetables, and herbs is a traditional Amish practice cherished for its simplicity, practicality, and reliability in preserving the garden's bounty. Growing up Amish, I watched closely as my family transformed fresh produce into delicious, nutrient-rich dried foods that enhanced our meals year-round. Here, I'll share practical, proven Amish drying techniques to help you successfully preserve fruits, vegetables, and herbs, maintaining vibrant color, excellent flavor, and nutritional benefits.

Best Amish Techniques for Drying Fruits

Dried fruits retain sweetness and nutrients, providing energy-rich snacks and versatile cooking ingredients.

Best Fruits for Drying:

- Apples, pears, peaches, apricots, cherries, grapes, strawberries, blueberries, bananas

Step-by-Step Fruit Drying Method:

Step 1: Preparing Fruits

- Select ripe but firm fruits without bruises.
- Wash thoroughly and pat completely dry.
- Remove cores, pits, and stems; slice evenly (¼-inch thick) for uniform drying.

Amish tip:
Soak sliced apples or pears briefly (5–10 minutes) in diluted lemon juice (¼ cup lemon juice to 2 cups water) to prevent browning.

Step 2: Drying the Fruits

- Spread fruit slices in single layers on drying screens or trays, ensuring no overlap.
- Dry fruits outdoors in full sun (covered with cheesecloth), in an oven at low temperatures (120–150°F / 50–65°C), or on drying racks near heat sources (woodstove/fireplace).
- Rotate trays and flip slices regularly (every few hours) for even drying.

Amish practical advice:
Fruits are fully dried when leathery, flexible, and slightly sticky to the touch. Apples and pears typically dry in 6–12 hours, berries and grapes 12–24 hours, and peaches or apricots around 8–16 hours.

Best Amish Techniques for Drying Vegetables

Properly dried vegetables retain nutrients, flavor, and versatility, perfect for soups, stews, and casseroles.

Best Vegetables for Drying:

- Beans, corn, carrots, onions, garlic, tomatoes, peppers, zucchini, potatoes, mushrooms

Step-by-Step Vegetable Drying Method:

Step 1: Preparing Vegetables

- Wash thoroughly, peel if desired, and remove stems or blemishes.
- Slice vegetables uniformly (¼-inch thick) for consistent drying.
- Blanch certain vegetables (beans, corn, carrots, potatoes) by boiling briefly (2–4 minutes) and immediately cooling in ice water to preserve color and nutrients.

Amish wisdom:
Blanching helps vegetables dry faster, prevents spoilage, and retains vibrant colors and nutrients—don't skip this step for dense vegetables.

Step 2: Drying the Vegetables

- Arrange vegetables in single layers on drying racks or trays, ensuring adequate airflow.
- Dry in direct sunlight, oven, or near a heat source at low temperatures (120–150°F / 50–65°C), turning regularly for even drying.
- Vegetables are fully dried when crisp, brittle, or leathery and break easily without moisture residue.

Amish practical tip:
Tomatoes, peppers, and mushrooms typically dry in 8–12 hours, whereas carrots, beans, potatoes, and corn may require 12–24 hours depending on thickness and drying method.

Best Amish Techniques for Drying Herbs

Herbs dried properly retain robust flavor and aroma, perfect for cooking, seasoning, and herbal remedies.

Best Herbs for Drying:

- Basil, oregano, sage, thyme, dill, mint, rosemary, lavender, parsley, chives

Step-by-Step Herb Drying Method:

Step 1: Harvesting and Preparing Herbs

- Harvest herbs in mid-morning after dew evaporates but before peak afternoon sun.
- Remove any damaged leaves and gently rinse herbs, drying completely with paper towels or cloth.

Amish practical tip:
Harvest herbs just before flowering for optimal essential oil and flavor retention.

Step 2: Bundling and Hanging Herbs

- Tie herbs into small bundles using cotton twine.
- Hang bundles upside-down indoors or outdoors in shaded, ventilated areas protected from direct sun and moisture.

- Dry herbs naturally for 2–7 days depending on leaf thickness and humidity.

Step 3: Testing and Storing Herbs

- Herbs are fully dried when leaves crumble easily and stems snap when bent.
- Strip leaves gently from stems and store in airtight containers away from heat and direct sunlight.

Amish wisdom:
Drying herbs slowly and gently preserves maximum flavor—avoid high heat or direct sunlight to retain herbs' aromatic properties.

Amish Practical Tips for Best Results Across All Foods:

- **Even Thickness:** Always slice fruits and vegetables uniformly to ensure consistent drying.
- **Airflow:** Arrange food in single, spaced-out layers to allow maximum air circulation.
- **Rotation:** Rotate trays or racks and gently turn food frequently to dry evenly.
- **Temperature Control:** Maintain low, consistent temperatures to dry foods gently without cooking or burning.

- **Proper Testing:** Test dryness thoroughly—fruits should be leathery, vegetables crisp, and herbs crumbly.

Traditional Amish Drying Troubleshooting:

- **Uneven Drying:**
  Rotate and turn items more frequently; rearrange trays or racks regularly.

- **Mold or Spoilage:**
  Ensure vegetables and fruits are sliced thinly enough, dried fully, and stored immediately once dry.

- **Loss of Flavor or Color:**
  Avoid excessive heat; use blanching and lemon juice treatments to preserve color and flavor.

Amish Quick Reference for Drying Times (Approximate):

Food	Drying Time (Typical)	Finished Texture
Apples, Pears	6–12 hours	Leathery, flexible
Berries, Grapes	12–24 hours	Slightly leathery, sticky
Carrots, Beans	12–24 hours	Dry, crisp, brittle
Tomatoes, Peppers	8–12 hours	Leathery, slightly brittle
Herbs	2–7 days	Dry, brittle, crumbly leaves

By applying these authentic Amish drying techniques, you'll confidently preserve fruits, vegetables, and herbs, maintaining flavor, nutrition, and usefulness year-round. Each batch of dried produce connects you to Amish tradition, enriches your cooking, and provides wholesome, delicious ingredients to nourish your family—just as generations of Amish homemakers have done before.

Common Drying Mistakes and Solutions

Food drying is a trusted tradition among Amish households for preserving the bounty of gardens and orchards. However, even experienced Amish homemakers occasionally encounter problems during drying. Growing up Amish, I learned practical, straightforward solutions to common drying issues, ensuring consistently successful outcomes. Here, I'll share traditional Amish wisdom and clear remedies to quickly identify and resolve common drying mistakes.

Mistake 1: Unevenly Dried Foods

Possible Causes:

- Fruits or vegetables sliced unevenly
- Insufficient turning or rotation during drying
- Crowded or overlapping items on drying trays

Amish Solutions:

- Slice produce evenly, approximately ¼-inch thick for consistent drying.
- Rotate trays regularly and flip food pieces every few hours.
- Space foods adequately on drying racks, allowing sufficient airflow around each piece.

Amish Practical Tip:
Consistent rotation is essential—Amish families traditionally turn drying foods at least every 2–3 hours to ensure uniform dryness.

Mistake 2: Foods Taking Too Long to Dry

Possible Causes:

- Pieces cut too thickly or unevenly
- High humidity or inadequate airflow
- Low drying temperatures or poor heat source

Amish Solutions:

- Slice foods thinner (around ⅛–¼ inch) to accelerate drying times.
- Improve airflow by increasing tray spacing or adding gentle fans indoors.
- Dry foods at slightly higher yet safe temperatures (120–150°F / 50–65°C).

Amish Wisdom:
Humidity greatly affects drying—choose dry, sunny days for outdoor drying, or enhance indoor airflow for efficient results.

Mistake 3: Mold or Spoilage During Drying

Possible Causes:

- Drying in overly humid conditions
- Insufficient airflow
- Fruits and vegetables dried too slowly

Amish Solutions:

- Increase airflow by spreading foods thinly and evenly, avoiding overlap.
- Use fans indoors or dry outdoors on sunny, low-humidity days.
- Slice produce thinner to ensure quicker drying and reduce spoilage risk.

Amish Practical Advice:
Immediately discard moldy or spoiled food—no amount of further drying will safely remove mold or spoilage once present.

Mistake 4: Foods Becoming Too Hard or Brittle

Possible Causes:

- Overdrying due to excessive heat or prolonged drying times
- Thinly sliced food dried longer than necessary

Amish Solutions:

- Regularly test dryness throughout the drying process; remove promptly once fully dried.
- Rehydrate slightly over-dried fruits or vegetables by soaking briefly in warm water before use.

Amish Tip:
Monitor drying foods carefully; ideal textures are leathery (fruits), crisp (vegetables), or crumbly (herbs)—avoid overdrying.

Mistake 5: Poor Flavor or Unappealing Color

Possible Causes:

- High drying temperatures causing loss of flavor or browning
- Failure to blanch vegetables or pretreat fruits properly

Amish Solutions:

- Dry foods gently at lower, consistent temperatures (120–150°F / 50–65°C).
- Always blanch vegetables briefly before drying (especially beans, carrots, potatoes) to maintain flavor and vibrant color.
- Pretreat fruits in diluted lemon juice or ascorbic acid solution to prevent discoloration.

Amish Practical Wisdom:
Blanching and pretreatments significantly improve flavor retention and appearance—never skip these simple steps.

Mistake 6: Herbs Losing Flavor or Aroma

Possible Causes:

- Drying herbs in direct sunlight or high temperatures
- Overdrying herbs, leading to flavor loss

Amish Solutions:

- Always dry herbs slowly in shaded, airy areas away from direct sunlight.

- Dry herbs at room temperature or gentle warmth, never exceeding 100°F (38°C).
- Herbs are ready when leaves crumble easily; remove promptly to prevent flavor deterioration.

Amish Traditional Advice:
Slow, gentle drying preserves aromatic oils—key to herbs' flavorful potency.

Mistake 7: Insects or Pests Infesting Drying Foods

Possible Causes:

- Drying foods uncovered or inadequately protected outdoors
- Storage of dried foods without proper sealing or protection

Amish Solutions:

- Cover drying trays outdoors with lightweight cheesecloth or muslin, protecting from insects while allowing airflow.
- Store dried foods promptly in airtight containers, jars, or vacuum-sealed bags immediately after drying.

Amish Practical Tip:
Insects are attracted quickly—cover foods from the beginning of drying, not after infestation occurs.

Amish Quick Troubleshooting Reference:

Issue	Amish Quick Solution
Uneven Drying	Rotate trays often, slice evenly
Slow Drying	Improve airflow, slice thinner, dry in lower humidity
Mold or Spoilage	Increase airflow, thinner slicing, discard moldy items
Too Hard or Brittle	Test frequently, avoid overdrying

Poor Flavor or Color	Blanch vegetables, pretreat fruits, lower drying temperature
Herbs Losing Aroma	Dry gently, away from sunlight and heat, remove promptly
Insect or Pest Issues	Cover drying trays, store dried foods sealed immediately

Amish Practical Checklist for Avoiding Drying Mistakes:

- ✓ Slice foods evenly and thinly
- ✓ Maintain good airflow and proper spacing
- ✓ Rotate drying trays and turn food regularly
- ✓ Dry at appropriate, gentle temperatures
- ✓ Pretreat fruits and blanch vegetables properly
- ✓ Monitor regularly, removing food promptly once fully dry
- ✓ Store dried foods immediately in airtight containers

By recognizing and correcting these common drying mistakes through traditional Amish methods and practical solutions, you'll achieve successful, safe, and delicious results consistently. Each successful batch of dried fruits, vegetables, or herbs will nourish your family, preserve seasonal abundance, and connect you with the timeless Amish tradition of natural food preservation.

Practical Storage Tips for Dried Goods

Proper storage is the final, crucial step in preserving dried foods, ensuring they remain flavorful, nutritious, and safe. Amish families have perfected practical, reliable storage techniques through generations, allowing dried fruits, vegetables, and herbs to nourish their families year-round. Growing up Amish, I learned these traditional storage methods firsthand. In this guide, I'll share authentic Amish advice and clear, practical storage solutions to help you protect and preserve your dried foods at their best.

Ideal Storage Conditions for Dried Foods

Properly dried foods thrive when stored in the following ideal conditions:

- **Cool Temperatures:** Maintain storage areas between 50°F–60°F (10°C–16°C) for optimal freshness.

- **Low Humidity:** Humidity levels should be low (below 60%) to prevent moisture absorption and spoilage.
- **Darkness:** Protect dried foods from direct sunlight or bright lights to maintain color, flavor, and nutrients.
- **Air-tight Containers:** Store dried goods in tightly sealed containers to keep moisture, insects, and pests out.

Amish Practical Tip:
Basements, root cellars, pantries, or kitchen cupboards away from heat sources are traditional Amish storage spaces ideal for dried foods.

Best Amish-Recommended Storage Containers

Proper storage containers protect dried foods from spoilage, pests, and environmental exposure:

- **Glass Jars:**
  Mason jars or other glass jars with tight-fitting lids are preferred by Amish families for excellent visibility, easy labeling, and airtight sealing.
- **Vacuum-Sealed Bags or Containers:**
  Removing air using vacuum sealing significantly extends shelf-life and freshness of dried foods, preventing oxidation.
- **Metal or Ceramic Containers:**
  Containers with tight-fitting lids effectively block sunlight, moisture, and pests—perfect for dried herbs and delicate vegetables.
- **Food-Grade Plastic Containers:**
  Ensure containers are clean, food-safe, airtight, and BPA-free for reliable, economical storage.

Amish Practical Advice:
Clearly label each container with its contents and drying date—simplifying inventory management and proper food rotation.

Storing Dried Fruits the Amish Way

- Ensure fruits are completely dry (leathery, flexible, not sticky).

- Pack dried fruits tightly into jars or vacuum-sealed bags, leaving minimal air space.
- Store in cool, dark locations; for long-term storage (more than 6 months), refrigeration or freezing extends freshness.

Amish tip:
For extra protection against moisture, place small food-safe silica gel packets or oxygen absorbers inside containers with dried fruits.

Storing Dried Vegetables Amish-Style

- Vegetables should be thoroughly dried (crisp, brittle, easily snapped) before storage.
- Pack vegetables tightly into airtight containers or vacuum-sealed bags, removing as much air as possible.
- Store dried vegetables away from sunlight, heat, and humidity, ideally below 60°F (16°C).

Amish practical advice:
For extended storage (up to 1–2 years), consider freezing dried vegetables—this significantly maintains their flavor, color, and nutrients.

Proper Storage for Dried Herbs (Traditional Amish Method)

- Herbs must be fully dried and crumbly before storing.
- Store dried herbs whole or gently crushed in airtight containers (glass jars or ceramic containers) in cool, dark cupboards.
- Keep herbs away from heat sources, moisture, and direct sunlight to preserve flavor and aromatic properties.

Amish wisdom:
Store herbs in small, labeled jars—open frequently only what you'll use quickly, keeping larger batches sealed to retain maximum flavor.

Preventing and Managing Pests—Amish Practical Solutions

Protect dried foods from pests and insects through preventative measures:

- Regularly inspect containers for insect activity, discarding any contaminated batches immediately.
- Store dried foods in airtight containers, minimizing chances of infestation.
- Use natural repellents (bay leaves or mint leaves) placed inside pantry cupboards or containers to deter pests safely and naturally.

Amish traditional advice:
Bay leaves added to storage containers or pantry shelves help naturally repel insects and pests, a time-tested Amish secret.

Shelf-Life Reference—Traditional Amish Guidelines

When properly dried and stored, foods typically maintain optimal quality as follows:

Dried Food Type	Shelf-Life (Properly Stored)	Ideal Storage Conditions
Fruits	6–12 months (pantry), 1–2 years refrigerated/frozen	Airtight, cool, dark location
Vegetables	1–2 years refrigerated/frozen	Airtight, cool, low humidity
Herbs	1–2 years	Airtight, dark, dry, cool place

Recognizing Spoilage in Dried Foods—Amish Wisdom

Regularly inspect dried foods, trusting your senses for signs of spoilage:

- **Visual:**
  Mold growth, discoloration, or unusual textures indicate spoilage—discard immediately.
- **Smell:**
  Musty, off odors, or rancidity clearly signal spoilage—do not consume.

- **Texture:**
  Unexpected softness, stickiness, or dampness indicates moisture contamination—discard promptly.

Amish Practical Tip:
When in doubt, discard questionable dried goods—safety and quality always take priority.

Amish Quick Reference Checklist for Proper Dried Food Storage:

- ✓ Maintain cool, dry, dark storage conditions (50°F–60°F / 10°C–16°C).
- ✓ Use airtight containers (glass jars, vacuum bags, metal tins).
- ✓ Label containers clearly with contents and drying date.
- ✓ Regularly inspect stored foods for freshness and spoilage.
- ✓ Rotate dried foods consistently ("first-in, first-out").

CHAPTER 6: AMISH ROOT CELLARING BASICS

How to Build and Organize a Simple Root Cellar

Root cellaring is a cherished tradition among Amish families, providing an effective, natural way to store garden produce safely through winter months. Growing up Amish, my family relied heavily on our root cellar, turning a simple underground space into a year-round pantry full of flavorful, nutritious vegetables and fruits. In this practical guide, I'll help you build and organize your own simple, effective root cellar, sharing authentic Amish methods, step-by-step instructions, and practical tips to maximize your storage space, protect your produce, and ensure freshness.

Why Build a Root Cellar? Traditional Amish Wisdom

A root cellar offers several key benefits:

- **Natural refrigeration** without electricity or artificial cooling.
- **Long-term storage** for root vegetables, fruits, and canned goods.
- **Cost-effective preservation** using stable, natural earth temperatures.
- **Food security** by keeping produce fresh and accessible year-round.

Step-by-Step Guide to Building a Simple Amish Root Cellar

Step 1: Choosing the Ideal Location

Amish root cellars are traditionally built into hillsides, partially underground, or beneath homes for natural insulation.

- Select a site slightly elevated or sloped, allowing water drainage.
- North-facing slopes typically provide cooler, more stable temperatures.
- If not hillside, consider beneath porch areas or in corners of basements, ensuring good drainage and ventilation.

Step 2: Planning Your Cellar Size and Layout

Simple Amish cellars typically measure around 6 to 8 feet wide, 8 to 10 feet long, and 6 to 7 feet tall—large enough for shelves, bins, and easy access.

- Design to accommodate shelving along walls for maximum storage.
- Include central open space for easy access and ventilation.

Step 3: Digging and Preparing Your Root Cellar

- Dig or excavate space to desired dimensions, ensuring walls are stable and sloped slightly outward for structural safety.
- Level the floor and ensure adequate drainage—gravel flooring or a drain pipe channeling excess moisture outside is common Amish practice.
- Line walls with cinder blocks, bricks, stones, or untreated wooden planks for stability and moisture control.

Amish practical tip:
If built beneath a home or structure, reinforce walls and ceilings safely and adequately to support overhead weight.

Step 4: Building the Cellar Entrance and Doorway

- Frame the entrance with sturdy wooden or stone walls to maintain structural integrity.
- Install a strong, insulated, well-fitted wooden door to maintain stable temperatures and prevent pests or drafts.
- Include weatherstripping or tight-fitting seals around doors for added temperature and moisture control.

Amish traditional advice:
Your cellar door should always remain tightly closed except when accessing food—maintaining stable conditions is critical for storage longevity.

Step 5: Ensuring Proper Ventilation

Good airflow prevents mold, spoilage, and odors, essential in any Amish root cellar.

- Install two ventilation pipes—one near the ceiling (to allow warm air escape) and one near the floor (to bring cooler air inside).
- Use simple PVC or metal pipes, screened or capped to prevent pests from entering.
- Cover vent openings outside with wire mesh or screens.

Amish wisdom:
Ventilation pipes placed diagonally opposite each other significantly enhance natural airflow, maintaining optimal freshness.

Step 6: Adding Storage Shelves, Bins, and Containers

Organized storage maximizes your root cellar's efficiency:

- Install sturdy shelves along walls for canned goods, pickles, and dried foods.
- Place wooden crates, bins, or baskets on the floor for root vegetables (potatoes, carrots, onions).
- Use hanging mesh bags or nets suspended from ceilings for onions, garlic, or apples, maximizing space and airflow.

Amish practical advice:
Wooden crates or ventilated bins allow air circulation, reducing spoilage and extending freshness significantly.

Step 7: Controlling Humidity (Traditional Amish Methods)

Root cellars ideally maintain 80%–95% humidity for root vegetables and slightly lower for fruits:

- Spread dampened sand or sawdust on cellar floors or in bins to increase humidity naturally.
- Place buckets or shallow pans filled with water inside if humidity feels too low.
- Conversely, improve ventilation or add dry straw if humidity feels excessive.

Amish practical tip:
Adjust humidity gradually and monitor closely; a simple hygrometer is a helpful tool.

Amish Root Cellar Organization—Practical Tips

- **Root Vegetables (potatoes, carrots, beets):**
  Store in bins layered with sand or sawdust, maintaining moisture, freshness, and preventing spoilage.

- **Onions and Garlic:**
  Store in mesh bags, baskets, or hung in bunches from ceiling beams, ensuring airflow and dryness.

- **Apples and Pears:**
  Store in crates or bins separately, checking regularly for spoilage, as fruit gases accelerate vegetable spoilage.

- **Cabbage and Squash:**
  Store on shelves or in crates with adequate airflow, inspecting regularly.

- **Canned and Pickled Goods:**
  Arrange jars neatly on shelves, clearly labeled and rotated regularly ("first-in, first-out").

Amish Safety and Maintenance Checklist for Your Root Cellar:

- ✓ Regularly inspect for spoilage, pests, and mold.
- ✓ Monitor temperature (ideal: 32°F–50°F / 0°C–10°C).
- ✓ Maintain humidity levels (80%–95% for vegetables).
- ✓ Ensure proper ventilation and airflow.
- ✓ Keep cellar door tightly closed and well-sealed.

Common Amish Root Cellar Storage Durations (Approximate):

Produce Type	Ideal Storage Duration	Optimal Conditions
Potatoes	4–8 months	Cool, dark, humid (90%)
Carrots, Beets	4–6 months	Humid, layered in damp sand
Onions, Garlic	4–8 months	Dry, ventilated, cool
Apples, Pears	2–4 months	Cool, slightly humid
Cabbage, Squash	3–6 months	Cool, moderate humidity
Pickled/Canned	1–2 years	Dark, cool, dry shelves

Ideal Conditions for Long-Term Storage

Amish families have long understood the importance of carefully maintaining ideal conditions in their root cellars, enabling produce to stay fresh, flavorful, and nutritious through long winters. Growing up Amish, I learned that simply storing vegetables and fruits underground isn't enough—true success relies on carefully managing temperature, humidity, ventilation, and darkness. In this practical guide, I'll share authentic Amish wisdom to help you maintain the ideal conditions in your root cellar, ensuring your produce remains safe and delicious for months of successful storage.

The Four Key Elements of Root Cellar Storage

Effective long-term storage in an Amish root cellar requires controlling these four essential conditions:

1. **Temperature**
2. **Humidity**
3. **Ventilation**
4. **Darkness**

1. Ideal Temperature for Amish Root Cellars

Proper temperature control is crucial for maintaining freshness and preventing spoilage. Amish root cellars typically maintain stable temperatures between **32°F and 50°F (0°C–10°C)**.

- **Root Vegetables (Potatoes, Carrots, Beets):**
  Best at cooler temperatures around 32°F–40°F (0°C–4°C).

- **Fruits (Apples, Pears):**
  Slightly warmer temperatures between 35°F–45°F (2°C–7°C).

- **Onions, Garlic, Squash:**
  Optimal temperatures around 40°F–50°F (4°C–10°C).

Amish Practical Tip:
Place thermometers in multiple locations within the cellar, regularly checking and adjusting ventilation or insulation as needed to maintain stable temperatures.

2. Ideal Humidity Levels (Traditional Amish Method)

Proper humidity significantly impacts produce freshness and longevity:

- **Root Vegetables (Potatoes, Carrots, Beets, Turnips):**
  Require high humidity—approximately **85%–95%**. Higher moisture helps retain texture, preventing shriveling and softening.

- **Apples, Pears, Cabbage, Squash:**
  Moderate humidity—around **80%–90%**—to prevent shriveling without promoting mold growth.

- **Onions and Garlic:**
  Require low humidity—around **60%–70%**. High humidity causes mold and spoilage.

Amish Wisdom:
Simple methods like placing damp sand or sawdust beneath vegetables can naturally increase humidity, while dry straw or improved ventilation helps reduce humidity.

3. Proper Ventilation and Air Circulation

Proper airflow prevents spoilage, mold growth, and off-flavors. Amish root cellars traditionally incorporate natural ventilation:

- **Install Two Ventilation Pipes:**
    - One vent near the floor (brings cool air in)
    - Another vent near the ceiling (allows warm, moist air to escape)

- **Natural Airflow:**
  Pipes positioned diagonally opposite promote gentle, consistent airflow without creating temperature fluctuations.

- **Prevent Drafts:**
  Good ventilation doesn't mean strong drafts—air movement should be gentle yet continuous.

Amish Practical Advice:
Cover outdoor vent openings with screens or mesh to keep pests out while allowing consistent airflow.

4. Maintaining Darkness

Complete darkness is essential for preserving freshness, preventing sprouting, and protecting nutrient content:

- Avoid windows or light sources inside root cellars; use insulated doors.
- Use wooden crates, shelves, or opaque containers for produce storage, adding extra darkness and protection.

Amish Practical Tip:
If entering your root cellar regularly, consider a small portable lantern or flashlight rather than permanent lighting to minimize unnecessary exposure to light.

Amish Ideal Conditions Reference Chart

Produce Type	Ideal Temperature	Ideal Humidity	Optimal Storage Tips
Potatoes, Carrots, Beets	32°F–40°F (0°C–4°C)	85%–95%	Store in bins layered with damp sand/sawdust
Apples, Pears	35°F–45°F (2°C–7°C)	80%–90%	Store separately to reduce spoilage from gases
Onions, Garlic	40°F–50°F (4°C–10°C)	60%–70%	Hang or store in mesh bags for ventilation
Cabbage, Squash	35°F–45°F (2°C–7°C)	80%–90%	Store on shelves with adequate airflow

Maintaining Ideal Conditions: Amish Troubleshooting Guide

Problem: Temperatures Too Warm

- **Solution:**
  Improve ventilation to release warm air, ensure cellar door seals tightly, or add insulation.

Problem: Temperatures Too Cold (Below Freezing)

- **Solution:**
  Add insulation around cellar door, partially block lower ventilation pipe temporarily, or use straw insulation.

Problem: Humidity Too High (Mold Issues)

- **Solution:**
  Increase ventilation, add dry straw, or temporarily use moisture absorbers (baking soda, charcoal).

Problem: Humidity Too Low (Shriveling Produce)

- **Solution:**
  Introduce damp sand or containers of water to naturally raise humidity levels.

Amish Checklist for Maintaining Ideal Storage Conditions:

- ✓ Regularly check temperatures (32°F–50°F / 0°C–10°C) with accurate thermometers.
- ✓ Monitor humidity levels (60%–95%) and adjust naturally as needed.
- ✓ Ensure gentle, consistent ventilation and airflow.
- ✓ Maintain complete darkness inside root cellar.
- ✓ Inspect regularly for spoilage, adjusting conditions promptly.

Ideal Conditions for Long-Term Storage

Amish families have long understood the importance of carefully maintaining ideal conditions in their root cellars, enabling produce to stay fresh, flavorful, and nutritious through long winters. Growing up Amish, I learned that simply storing vegetables and fruits underground isn't enough—true success relies on carefully managing temperature, humidity, ventilation, and darkness. In this practical guide, I'll share authentic Amish wisdom to help you maintain the ideal conditions in your root cellar, ensuring your produce remains safe and delicious for months of successful storage.

The Four Key Elements of Root Cellar Storage

Effective long-term storage in an Amish root cellar requires controlling these four essential conditions:

1. **Temperature**
2. **Humidity**
3. **Ventilation**
4. **Darkness**

1. Ideal Temperature for Amish Root Cellars

Proper temperature control is crucial for maintaining freshness and preventing spoilage. Amish root cellars typically maintain stable temperatures between **32°F and 50°F (0°C–10°C)**.

- **Root Vegetables (Potatoes, Carrots, Beets):**
  Best at cooler temperatures around 32°F–40°F (0°C–4°C).

- **Fruits (Apples, Pears):**
  Slightly warmer temperatures between 35°F–45°F (2°C–7°C).

- **Onions, Garlic, Squash:**
  Optimal temperatures around 40°F–50°F (4°C–10°C).

Amish Practical Tip:
Place thermometers in multiple locations within the cellar, regularly checking and adjusting ventilation or insulation as needed to maintain stable temperatures.

2. Ideal Humidity Levels (Traditional Amish Method)

Proper humidity significantly impacts produce freshness and longevity:

- **Root Vegetables (Potatoes, Carrots, Beets, Turnips):**
  Require high humidity—approximately **85%–95%**. Higher moisture helps retain texture, preventing shriveling and softening.

- **Apples, Pears, Cabbage, Squash:**
  Moderate humidity—around **80%–90%**—to prevent shriveling without promoting mold growth.

- **Onions and Garlic:**
  Require low humidity—around **60%–70%**. High humidity causes mold and spoilage.

Amish Wisdom:
Simple methods like placing damp sand or sawdust beneath vegetables can naturally increase humidity, while dry straw or improved ventilation helps reduce humidity.

3. Proper Ventilation and Air Circulation

Proper airflow prevents spoilage, mold growth, and off-flavors. Amish root cellars traditionally incorporate natural ventilation:

- **Install Two Ventilation Pipes:**
  - One vent near the floor (brings cool air in)
  - Another vent near the ceiling (allows warm, moist air to escape)

- **Natural Airflow:**
  Pipes positioned diagonally opposite promote gentle, consistent airflow without creating temperature fluctuations.

- **Prevent Drafts:**
  Good ventilation doesn't mean strong drafts—air movement should be gentle yet continuous.

Amish Practical Advice:
Cover outdoor vent openings with screens or mesh to keep pests out while allowing consistent airflow.

4. Maintaining Darkness

Complete darkness is essential for preserving freshness, preventing sprouting, and protecting nutrient content:

- Avoid windows or light sources inside root cellars; use insulated doors.
- Use wooden crates, shelves, or opaque containers for produce storage, adding extra darkness and protection.

Amish Practical Tip:
If entering your root cellar regularly, consider a small portable lantern or flashlight rather than permanent lighting to minimize unnecessary exposure to light.

Amish Ideal Conditions Reference Chart

Produce Type	Ideal Temperature	Ideal Humidity	Optimal Storage Tips
Potatoes, Carrots, Beets	32°F–40°F (0°C–4°C)	85%–95%	Store in bins layered with damp sand/sawdust
Apples, Pears	35°F–45°F (2°C–7°C)	80%–90%	Store separately to reduce spoilage from gases
Onions, Garlic	40°F–50°F (4°C–10°C)	60%–70%	Hang or store in mesh bags for ventilation
Cabbage, Squash	35°F–45°F (2°C–7°C)	80%–90%	Store on shelves with adequate airflow

Maintaining Ideal Conditions: Amish Troubleshooting Guide

Problem: Temperatures Too Warm

- **Solution:**
  Improve ventilation to release warm air, ensure cellar door seals tightly, or add insulation.

Problem: Temperatures Too Cold (Below Freezing)

- **Solution:**
  Add insulation around cellar door, partially block lower ventilation pipe temporarily, or use straw insulation.

Problem: Humidity Too High (Mold Issues)

- **Solution:**
  Increase ventilation, add dry straw, or temporarily use moisture absorbers (baking soda, charcoal).

Problem: Humidity Too Low (Shriveling Produce)

- **Solution:**
  Introduce damp sand or containers of water to naturally raise humidity levels.

Amish Checklist for Maintaining Ideal Storage Conditions:

- ✓ Regularly check temperatures (32°F–50°F / 0°C–10°C) with accurate thermometers.
- ✓ Monitor humidity levels (60%–95%) and adjust naturally as needed.
- ✓ Ensure gentle, consistent ventilation and airflow.
- ✓ Maintain complete darkness inside root cellar.
- ✓ Inspect regularly for spoilage, adjusting conditions promptly.

Practical Advice for Storing Root Vegetables and Fruits

In Amish communities, properly storing root vegetables and fruits is an essential skill that ensures garden-fresh produce remains nutritious, flavorful, and readily available throughout the long winter months. Growing up Amish, I learned simple yet highly effective storage practices that allowed our family to enjoy delicious fruits and vegetables long after harvest season ended. Here, I'll share practical, authentic Amish advice on storing root vegetables and fruits, enabling you to keep your produce fresh, crisp, and nutritious for months at a time.

Amish Practical Tips for Storing Root Vegetables

Potatoes – Traditional Amish Methods

- **Preparation:**
  Harvest potatoes carefully, avoiding bruises and cuts. Allow them to dry outdoors briefly (a few hours), gently brushing off excess dirt.
- **Storage Conditions:**
  Store potatoes in complete darkness at temperatures around 35°F–40°F (2°C–4°C) with high humidity (90%–95%).
- **Method:**
  Layer potatoes gently in wooden crates, bins, or ventilated baskets, ensuring good airflow. Never store near apples, onions, or pears (which produce gases accelerating sprouting or spoilage).

Amish practical tip:
Check regularly and remove sprouted or soft potatoes immediately to avoid spoiling the entire batch.

Carrots, Beets, and Parsnips – Authentic Amish Storage

- **Preparation:**
  Harvest carefully, removing leafy tops about ½-inch above roots. Gently remove excess soil without washing.
- **Storage Conditions:**
  Ideal storage temperature is 32°F–40°F (0°C–4°C) at 85%–95% humidity.
- **Method:**
  Layer carrots, beets, and parsnips in bins or wooden crates filled with damp sand or sawdust. Keep layers separated by sand or sawdust to maintain moisture and crispness.

Amish wisdom:
Regularly dampen the sand or sawdust slightly (never wet) to preserve freshness throughout storage.

Onions and Garlic – Amish Practical Advice

- **Preparation:**
  After harvest, cure onions and garlic bulbs outdoors or in ventilated sheds for 1–2 weeks, drying completely until skins become papery.

- **Storage Conditions:**
  Store onions and garlic in cool, dry conditions (35°F–50°F / 2°C–10°C) at lower humidity (60%–70%).

- **Method:**
  Hang bulbs in mesh bags, nets, or loosely woven baskets to promote airflow and prevent mold. Never store onions or garlic with potatoes or apples, as moisture or gases will accelerate spoilage.

Amish practical tip:
Inspect stored onions and garlic regularly, promptly discarding soft or sprouting bulbs to protect the remainder.

Cabbage – Amish Storage Method

- **Preparation:**
  Harvest cabbage by carefully removing loose outer leaves, leaving heads intact and unwashed.

- **Storage Conditions:**
  Store cabbage heads at temperatures between 32°F–40°F (0°C–4°C) with humidity around 85%–90%.

- **Method:**
  Store whole cabbage heads on ventilated shelves or in wooden crates with adequate spacing for airflow. For longer storage, wrap individual heads loosely in newspaper or place heads upside down, preventing moisture accumulation inside leaves.

Amish practical advice:
Remove any wilted or damaged outer leaves immediately during storage checks.

Squash and Pumpkins – Traditional Amish Storage Advice

- **Preparation:**
  After harvest, cure squash and pumpkins in warm, ventilated conditions (70°F–80°F / 21°C–27°C) for approximately 1–2 weeks to harden skins.

- **Storage Conditions:**
  Store in moderate humidity (70%–80%) at temperatures around 50°F–55°F (10°C–13°C).

- **Method:**
  Place squash and pumpkins on shelves or racks, keeping them slightly separated for good airflow. Avoid stacking or piling, which can cause bruising and encourage spoilage.

Amish wisdom:
Inspect regularly for soft spots, immediately using or discarding squash showing signs of decay to protect other stored vegetables.

Amish Practical Advice for Storing Fruits

Apples and Pears – Authentic Amish Method

- **Preparation:**
  Harvest fruits gently by hand, avoiding bruises. Select firm, slightly underripe fruits ideal for storage.

- **Storage Conditions:**
  Optimal storage temperatures for apples and pears range from 32°F–40°F (0°C–4°C) at 80%–90% humidity.

- **Method:**
  Store apples and pears individually wrapped in newspaper or separated by straw in ventilated bins or crates, arranged loosely to ensure airflow. Always store fruits separately from vegetables, especially potatoes and onions, to prevent accelerated ripening and spoilage.

Amish practical tip:
Check fruit storage frequently, removing any ripened or soft fruits immediately to prevent spoilage of the remaining batch.

Amish Practical Storage Duration Guide:

Produce	Storage Duration	Optimal Conditions & Method

Potatoes	4–8 months	Cool, dark, humid (90%–95%), ventilated bins/crates
Carrots, Beets	4–6 months	Layered in damp sand/sawdust, cool and humid
Onions, Garlic	4–8 months	Cool, dry (60%–70%), mesh bags/hanging
Cabbage	3–6 months	Cool, moist (85%–90%), shelves/crates
Squash, Pumpkins	3–6 months	Cool (50°F–55°F), moderate humidity, shelves/racks
Apples, Pears	2–4 months	Cool, slightly humid, wrapped individually

Amish Checklist for Successful Root Cellar Storage:

- ✓ Choose fresh, undamaged produce for storage.
- ✓ Carefully prepare vegetables and fruits for storage (removing tops, curing onions, etc.).
- ✓ Maintain ideal storage conditions (temperature, humidity, airflow).
- ✓ Regularly inspect stored produce, removing spoiled or damaged items immediately.
- ✓ Separate fruits from vegetables to prevent spoilage from gases.
- ✓ Clearly label and rotate produce frequently ("first-in, first-out").

Tips to Prevent Spoilage and Extend Storage Life

In Amish tradition, preventing spoilage and maximizing the storage life of fruits and vegetables is a critical part of successful root cellaring. Through generations, Amish families have developed simple, effective practices that significantly extend freshness, nutrition, and flavor, ensuring a steady supply of wholesome food throughout winter. Growing up Amish, I learned that careful planning, attention to detail, and regular maintenance make all the difference. Here, I'll share practical, authentic Amish tips to help you prevent spoilage and extend the storage life of your produce successfully.

1. Select Only High-Quality, Undamaged Produce

The foundation of successful long-term storage begins at harvest:

- Harvest fruits and vegetables carefully, avoiding bruises, cuts, or damage.
- Immediately set aside any imperfect produce for immediate consumption or processing, storing only firm, healthy items.

Amish Practical Advice:
One spoiled vegetable can ruin an entire batch—meticulous selection at the start prevents future spoilage problems.

2. Properly Prepare Produce Before Storage

Each type of produce requires specific preparation:

- **Root vegetables (carrots, beets, parsnips):**
  Gently remove leafy tops (leave about ½ inch), and brush off dirt without washing.
- **Potatoes:**
  Allow them to air-dry outdoors briefly to toughen skins before storage, gently removing excess dirt without washing.
- **Onions and garlic:**
  Cure thoroughly outdoors or in ventilated sheds until skins become dry and papery.

- **Squash and pumpkins:**
  Cure at warm temperatures (70°F–80°F / 21°C–27°C) for 1–2 weeks, toughening skins to protect during storage.

Amish Practical Tip:
Never wash produce intended for long-term storage; moisture increases spoilage risks significantly.

3. Maintain Ideal Temperature and Humidity

Controlling storage conditions dramatically reduces spoilage:

- Regularly monitor root cellar temperatures (optimal: 32°F–50°F / 0°C–10°C) with accurate thermometers.
- Adjust humidity carefully for specific produce:
    - High humidity (85%–95%) for root vegetables.
    - Moderate humidity (80%–90%) for apples, pears, cabbage, squash.
    - Lower humidity (60%–70%) for onions, garlic.

Amish Wisdom:
Use natural moisture controls—damp sand or sawdust to raise humidity, dry straw or increased ventilation to lower humidity.

4. Ensure Adequate Airflow and Ventilation

Good airflow is essential for preventing mold, spoilage, and odors:

- Install two ventilation pipes in your cellar (one near ceiling, one near floor) to maintain gentle, consistent airflow.
- Avoid crowding produce—adequate spacing on shelves and in bins significantly improves freshness and longevity.

Amish Practical Tip:
Check vents regularly for blockages or pests, keeping airflow consistent and unobstructed.

5. Regularly Inspect and Rotate Stored Produce

Consistent maintenance helps catch spoilage early:

- Regularly inspect all stored items, removing any soft, moldy, or spoiled produce immediately.
- Clearly label containers or bins with dates and contents, practicing proper rotation ("first-in, first-out").

Amish Traditional Advice:
Weekly inspections allow early detection of spoilage, greatly reducing the spread of decay.

6. Separate Fruits from Vegetables in Storage

Certain fruits (apples, pears) emit gases that accelerate ripening or spoilage of vegetables:

- Store fruits separately, ideally on separate shelves or in different cellar sections.
- If space is limited, store fruits in sealed or ventilated containers away from vegetables.

Amish Practical Wisdom:
Separation reduces spoilage significantly, keeping both fruits and vegetables fresh much longer.

7. Use Natural Anti-Spoilage Materials

Amish families traditionally rely on natural materials to reduce spoilage:

- **Damp Sand or Sawdust:**
  Keeps root vegetables moist, crisp, and protected.
- **Dry Straw:**
  Adds insulation, reduces humidity, and provides protective layers around delicate squash and pumpkins.
- **Newspaper or Paper Wrapping:**
  Protects apples, pears, cabbage, and other produce, preventing bruising and moisture buildup.

Amish Tip:
Line shelves or bins with clean straw or paper for added insulation and moisture control.

8. Control Light and Darkness

Darkness is crucial for freshness, flavor, and preventing unwanted sprouting or color changes:

- Store produce in opaque bins or cover shelves with cloth to protect from any accidental exposure to light.
- Minimize artificial lighting—use handheld lanterns or flashlights briefly during inspections.

Amish Practical Advice:
Constant darkness maintains produce freshness and significantly prolongs storage life.

Amish Quick Troubleshooting Reference for Storage Problems

Issue	Amish Solution and Prevention Measures
Mold or Rot	Increase airflow, reduce humidity, remove spoiled produce
Produce Sprouting Prematurely	Reduce cellar temperatures slightly, increase darkness
Vegetables Drying Out	Increase humidity, use damp sand or sawdust layers
Fruits Ripening Quickly	Separate fruits from vegetables, store fruits cooler
Insects or Pest Infestation	Improve seals, screen ventilation openings, regular inspection

Amish Ideal Storage Durations (When Conditions Are Met):

- **Potatoes, Beets, Carrots:** 4–8 months
- **Onions, Garlic:** 4–8 months
- **Cabbage, Squash, Pumpkins:** 3–6 months
- **Apples, Pears:** 2–4 months

Amish Checklist to Prevent Spoilage and Extend Storage Life:

- ✓ Harvest carefully; store only healthy, firm produce.
- ✓ Properly prepare produce (curing, brushing off dirt).
- ✓ Maintain consistent temperature and humidity.
- ✓ Ensure gentle but consistent airflow and ventilation.
- ✓ Regularly inspect and rotate stored produce.
- ✓ Store fruits separately from vegetables.
- ✓ Use natural materials (sand, sawdust, straw) for added protection.
- ✓ Maintain darkness to prevent sprouting and maintain freshness.

Common Root Cellar Problems and Solutions

Even the most carefully built Amish root cellar can occasionally face challenges. Growing up Amish, I observed how my family quickly identified and solved common root cellar problems through practical, simple solutions. Here, I'll share traditional Amish insights and clear guidance to help you promptly recognize, diagnose, and resolve common root cellar storage issues, ensuring your produce remains fresh and delicious all season.

Problem 1: Mold or Mildew Growth

Cause:

- Excessive humidity
- Poor airflow or ventilation
- Produce stored too tightly

Amish Solutions:

- Increase airflow by opening ventilation slightly wider.
- Add dry straw or sawdust to absorb excess moisture naturally.
- Rearrange stored items to improve airflow; remove spoiled or moldy produce immediately.

Amish Practical Tip:
Regularly wipe shelves and walls with a vinegar-water solution (1:1 ratio) to naturally inhibit mold growth.

Problem 2: Root Vegetables Sprouting Prematurely

Cause:

- Temperatures too warm
- Excessive humidity
- Exposure to light

Amish Solutions:

- Lower cellar temperatures slightly (ideal 32°F–40°F / 0°C–4°C).

- Ensure total darkness by sealing gaps around doors or windows.
- Improve ventilation slightly to reduce humidity.

Amish Practical Advice:
Check potatoes and other root vegetables weekly, removing and consuming those showing signs of sprouting first.

Problem 3: Produce Shriveling or Drying Out

Cause:

- Humidity too low
- Insufficient moisture around stored produce

Amish Solutions:

- Introduce damp sand or sawdust layers to maintain moisture.
- Place shallow pans or buckets of water inside the cellar to raise humidity.
- Ensure produce (especially root vegetables) is layered adequately in moist materials.

Amish Traditional Tip:
Amish families traditionally layer carrots, beets, and potatoes in damp sand to maintain moisture and prevent shriveling.

Problem 4: Infestation of Pests or Rodents

Cause:

- Poorly sealed cellar entrances
- Produce improperly stored or exposed
- Lack of regular inspections

Amish Solutions:

- Regularly inspect and seal entry points using mesh screens, caulk, or weatherstripping.
- Store produce in secure, ventilated containers or bins.

- Place natural deterrents (peppermint oil-soaked cotton balls, bay leaves) around the cellar to repel pests.

Amish Practical Wisdom:
Inspect your root cellar weekly to identify pest activity early, enabling swift action to prevent infestation.

Problem 5: Produce Freezing in Winter

Cause:
- Temperatures dropping below freezing
- Inadequate insulation or ventilation issues

Amish Solutions:
- Improve insulation by lining doors or walls with straw, blankets, or insulating panels.
- Partially close the lower ventilation pipe during extremely cold periods to retain warmth.
- Move produce to warmer areas within the cellar or raise off cold floors with wooden crates or pallets.

Amish Practical Tip:
During cold spells, Amish families traditionally add additional layers of straw or blankets around bins to provide extra insulation.

Problem 6: Fruits or Vegetables Spoiling Rapidly

Cause:
- Produce harvested or stored improperly
- Fruits stored near vegetables (gas emissions)
- Poor initial sorting (damaged or bruised produce)

Amish Solutions:
- Immediately remove any spoiled produce to prevent spreading decay.

- Store fruits separately from vegetables, ideally in separate areas of the cellar.
- Conduct regular inspections, removing soft or damaged items promptly.

Amish Traditional Advice:
Wrapping apples and pears individually in newspaper significantly reduces spoilage and gas exposure.

Problem 7: Unpleasant Odors Developing

Cause:

- Hidden spoiled or rotting produce
- Poor ventilation causing stagnant air

Amish Solutions:

- Inspect thoroughly and remove spoiled or decaying items immediately.
- Increase airflow through ventilation adjustments temporarily.
- Sprinkle baking soda in open containers around cellar shelves or bins to naturally absorb odors.

Amish Practical Tip:
Regularly airing out your root cellar during warmer, dry days helps prevent unpleasant odors.

Amish Quick Troubleshooting Reference:

Issue	Amish Quick Solution
Mold or Mildew	Improve airflow, reduce humidity, vinegar-water cleaning
Sprouting Vegetables	Lower temperature, total darkness, better ventilation

Produce Drying Out	Increase humidity, add damp sand/sawdust
Pests or Rodents	Seal entry points, use natural deterrents
Freezing Produce	Improve insulation, reduce airflow temporarily
Rapid Spoilage	Separate fruits from vegetables, regular inspection
Unpleasant Odors	Increase ventilation, baking soda, remove spoiled produce

Amish Preventive Checklist for Root Cellar Problems:

- ✓ Regularly monitor temperature and humidity levels.
- ✓ Ensure consistent airflow and adequate ventilation.
- ✓ Inspect stored produce weekly, promptly removing spoiled items.
- ✓ Separate fruits and vegetables during storage.
- ✓ Seal entry points carefully to prevent pests.
- ✓ Use natural humidity and moisture controls (sand, straw, sawdust).
- ✓ Maintain total darkness to prevent premature sprouting.
- ✓ Keep cellar clean and organized at all times.

www.ingramcontent.com/pod-product-compliance
Lightning Source LLC
Chambersburg PA
CBHW050637160426
43194CB00010B/1702